The Road to Big Brother

One Man's Struggle Against
the Surveillance Society

By Ross Clark

ENCOUNTER BOOKS  NEW YORK · LONDON

Originally published in the UK by Harriman House Ltd in 2007
under the title "The Road to Southend Pier"
www.harriman-house.com

First American edition published in 2009 by Encounter Books,
an activity of Encounter for Culture and Education, Inc.,
a nonprofit, tax exempt corporation.
Encounter Books website address: www.encounterbooks.com

Manufactured in the United States and printed on
acid-free paper. The paper used in this publication meets
the minimum requirements of ANSI/NISO Z39.48 1992
(R 1997) (Permanence of Paper).

FIRST AMERICAN EDITION

LIBRARY OF CONGRESS CATALOGING-IN-PUBLICATION DATA
Clark, Ross.
The road to big brother : one man's struggle against the surveillance society / by Ross Clark.
p. cm.
Prev. ed.: The road to southend pier. 2007
Includes bibliographical references and index.
ISBN-13: 978-1-59403-248-6 (hardcover : alk. paper)
ISBN-10: 1-59403-248-3 (hardcover : alk. paper)
1. Privacy, Right of–Great Britain.
2. Electronic surveillance–Political aspects–Great Britain.
3. Electronic surveillance–Social aspects–Great Britain.
4. Electronic surveillance–Great Britain–Humor. I. Clark, Ross. Road to southend pier. II. Title.
JC596.2.G7C48 2009
323.44'820941–dc22
2008048051

THE SURVEILLANCE STATE, NOT THE "COMPETENCE STATE"

More than any other nation, modern Britain has moved closer to becoming the Panopticon State. As Ross Clark admirably demonstrates, the proliferation of security cameras, computerized databases, government-deputized private security forces, and mandatory disclosures has produced a degree of intrusivveness that Britons of just a few decades ago would have regarded as unacceptable, and even unthinkable.

Yet for all its pervasiveness, the system has a characteristic that Clark makes poignantly clear. As intrusive and pervasive as all this surveillance is, it shares another characteristic of big government programs as well: It is incompetent. Though cameras are everywhere, the images are so poor that criminals often escape detection; and when criminals actually are detected, they often escape because of loopholes in criminal procedure or privacy law that turn out to give criminals a pass even as ordinary citizens are increasingly constrained. The government seems more interested in deploying cameras than in actually controlling crime.

Indeed, the miserably ineffective record of Britain's closed-circuit cameras in stopping terrorists and catching criminals suggests that, whatever the justification, the government's enthusiasm stems from other purposes. But what could those be? Science fiction author Charles Stross wrote a novel, *The Atrocity Archives*, in which the proliferation of the cameras was explained by their ability to be weaponized in preparation for a space invasion. That explanation, alas, sounds more rational than what is going on. Or is the purpose simply to undermine people's feelings of independence and autonomy? Or is this merely a reflection of bureaucrats' desire—explored in detail by James Scott in his book *Seeing Like a State*—for the kind of perfect information that will allow them to address the messy confusion of the real world with arid precision? As Scott notes, such efforts always fail, and Ross Clark's account of Britain's surveillance society suggests that Britain is well on the way to proving Scott right yet again.

Americans, however, would be well-advised not to feel too secure themselves. Despite widespread opposition from drivers, American municipalities are already deploying cameras designed to catch drivers who run red lights or exceed speed limits. (The cameras generally lose when they come up for a vote, so politicians make sure that that doesn't happen). The interest here seems to be revenue more than safety.

First rolled out in the 1960s, stoplight cameras went digital in the 1990s. Now, these cameras are in use in over 100 communities in 20 states and the District of Columbia. Cameras aimed at catching speeders, already common in Britain and other countries, are beginning to be deployed in the United States as well. The technology is pretty simple—just a fixed camera with a sensor and a connection to the traffic signal or a radar gun. But the problems they present are much more complicated.

Some people just don't like the idea of being watched. Being monitored and punished at the behest of a law-enforcement robot sounds like something out of a science fiction movie, and not an especially cheerful one either.

Others worry about safety. Stoplight cameras are supposed to make us safer by discouraging drivers from running red lights. The trouble is that they work too well. Numerous studies have found that when these cameras are put in place, rear-end collisions increase dramatically. Drivers who once might have stretched the light a bit now slam on their brakes for fear of getting a ticket, with predictable results. A study of stoplight cameras in Washington, D.C. by *The Washington Post* found that despite producing more than 500,000 tickets (and generating over $32 million in revenue), stoplight cameras didn't reduce injuries or collisions. In fact, the number of accidents *increased* at the camera-equipped intersections.

This has generated a backlash, with some jurisdictions eliminating speed and stoplight cameras in response to complaints from the public. But these traffic cameras, though irritating, are primarily money machines for local jurisdictions, and their Big Brother potential is comparatively small.

Small, at least, compared to the softball-sized license-plate readers mounted atop some Maryland State Police cars. These cameras, coupled with sophisticated software, can read the license plates of any cars they see, and then automatically match plates against the state's motor vehicle database. Originally, this technology was deployed to find stolen cars, but now, predictably enough, it's being used to catch people who failed emissions tests, don't have adequate insurance, or have unpaid parking tickets. But what's really troubling is that there's nothing to stop such cameras from simply recording the license plate numbers and matching them up to a geographic database, so that the government can track the movements of citizens who have done nothing wrong. It requires little effort to imagine scenarios in which such a database could be put to nefarious use—tracking, for example, the movements of political opponents in the hopes of finding evidence of extramarital affairs, or even tipping off corrupt police officers or politicians that they are under investigation by other law enforcement agencies.

Not quite as reliable, yet, are the closed-circuit television cameras that are beginning to infest America's public spaces, as they have already done in Europe. Though face-recognition technology promises to let them track people as easily as the license-plate cameras track vehicles, so far that promise remains largely unmet: Face recognition is just too unreliable, so far. That is likely to change over time, though, and as these cameras proliferate the risks will grow: It's possible that all of your movements will be added to a database, and matched against the movement of others, allowing authorities to find out all sorts of things that are none of their business. You'll be lucky if they merely milk the database for revenue, as they've done with the speed cameras.

It's even worse online, of course. Although the internet allows a modicum of what might be called "nuisance-level" anonymity—if you post an insulting comment on someone's chat board, they probably won't be able to find you—it also allows those with more resources the ability to track pretty much everything you do and everywhere you go. People are already accustomed to their bosses snooping on their work-time browsing habits, but ISPs, advertisers, and others are tracking your leisure-time browsing, too, and their records are readily discoverable, in most cases, by state and federal authorities and even sometimes by private litigants.

Public surveillance is also hybridizing with private surveillance. I just received a PR email for a product called MethShield™, which helps pharmacists track purchasers of pseudoephedrine—a common cold remedy that is now restricted because it can be used, in quantity, to manufacture methamphetamine—so that purchases from a wide variety of drug stores can be indexed to the same individual. According to the pitch, an optional feature of the product is to alert the pharmacist of suspicious customer behavior:

> MethShield™ can tell you if the person at your counter is making their first visit to the pharmacy today or their fifteenth. The real power of MethShield™ comes with aggregation of the data. By taking the information you have entered and combining that with data from pharmacies across a state or nation, law enforcement can be provided with a real-time snapshot of any suspicious behavior. MethShield™ then provides law enforcement with a sophisticated set of intelligence tools to assist in the tracking and apprehension of potential pseudoephedrine runners.

Pharmacists don't just work for you anymore. They don't even just work for you and your insurance company. They work for you, your insurance company, and big government—and not necessarily in that order.

The result of all of this probably *won't* be an Orwellian nightmare. That's because Orwell's bureaucrats were far more dedicated than their real-world counterparts are likely to be. Indeed, one of the greatest contributions of Clark's work is his demonstration of how the entire surveillance operation doesn't really live up to the hype when it comes to its supposed reasons for existence, such as catching terrorists or preventing crime. Like any system operated by those with safe jobs and no direct stake in the outcome, the surveillance society, as it actually exists, seems to be more about creating the *appearance* of security than about the reality. Instead, the result will probably be more of a Kafkaesque nightmare, which may or may not come as a relief.

But while those who suffer from allergies or frequent colds may have to worry about being categorized as "pseudoephedrine runners"—a criminal category that didn't exist until a few years ago—this will no doubt be offset by the fact that most of the real criminals will escape unscathed. And that is another important lesson from Clark's book. While gathering information is often done in the name of preventing or solving crime, actually going out and *doing anything* about crime seems often to be too much trouble for law enforcement, which is too busy looking at telescreen images to be bothered with anything as messy and troublesome as actually arresting people who threaten the lives and property of others. Most of the surveillance apparatus is a Potemkin construction, easily evaded or simply ignored by criminals, and offering little relief to victims of robbery, burglary, or identity theft who look for action from the police. (This is especially the case since, as *Consumer Reports* recently noted, if you're a victim of identity theft it's likely because some government agency lost your data to hacking, insider fraud, or a misplaced laptop.)

This should come as no surprise. Protection from crime may be a priority to citizens, but the government's priority is gathering information and exercising control. Protecting citizens is somewhere further down the list. That has been the British experience, as Clark notes, and only the fact that many law enforcement officials in the America are directly elected is likely to mitigate against a similar outcome in the US.

So what should Americans do about this? First, read this book, which provides an excellent overview of the phenomenon, and of the warning provided by the experience of Britain, which is considerably farther down this particular slippery slope. Second, recognize that there's probably not that much we can do to maintain old-fashioned privacy. Privacy as we understand it is a relatively modern phenomenon, made possible when the technology of living (including such innovations as apartment buildings and automobiles, which made it hard for busybodies to keep track of individuals) outpaced the technology of prying. For most of human history, people lived in small tribes or villages where everyone knew everyone else's business. Increasingly, the future is looking like that past. Cameras are tiny and ubiquitous enough that no ban could possibly succeed, and the computers that allow individually innocuous bits of information to be aggregated into a data picture that tells a lot about you—and even your friends—are getting cheaper and more capable by the day.

One difference, however, is that in the old days, the big shots didn't have any more privacy than the rest of us. But—again, as Clark notes—the spread of security cameras is being matched by an increase in restrictions on photography, and efforts to limit the information available to ordinary citizens. If we are to see freedom and democracy flourish in the 21st century, we must insist that the elites are scrutinized just as much by the public as the reverse. That will be a tall enough order, I think.

GLENN REYNOLDS
January 2009

zipper, the voices of Jagger and Woody ring out in my ears—"Hey, don't you dare piss on our town"—followed by a swoop by Northampton's finest cops and, for me, a night in the cells? Would I end up like the teenage girls who, to round off a day out in Worthing in August 2007, decided to expose their breasts to the town's CCTV cameras and were threatened with prosecution as a result?

My doubts were raised when I learned that besides Jagger and Woody, I might find myself admonished by a five-year-old. The towns chosen by the government to have the talking cameras installed were trying to recruit primary school children for the task of shaming the nation's drunks and louts. Competitions were being organized to find children with the finest—or perhaps most nannying—voices. The winners, in the manner of Stalin's Russia, would then be recruited to keep wayward grown-ups on the straight and narrow.

Or would they? Was the Home Office really planning to staff CCTV control rooms with five-year-olds who would be expected to sit up until after midnight surveying banks of screens of vomiting, urinating louts, and shrilly berating them? I thought it unlikely—and I was right. Of course, what the children were being recruited to do was to make a series of pre-recorded messages. The more I delved, the less it came to sound like the cutting edge of crime-fighting.

I arrive in Northampton's largely deserted Market Square at 10 p.m. on a Tuesday evening with a full bladder—and much apprehension. Where are these cameras, and what are they going to say to me? "Excuse me, Sir, that's a litter bin, not a lavatory"? "Oi, you! Do up your f***ing zipper, you f***ing f***!"? And if I don't comply, how long will it take the cops to get to me? I find a lamp-post, affixed with a loudspeaker and a prominent notice warning "CCTV radio watch area." Nervously, I unzip. Then, after half a minute hosing away, up I zip again. And off I go.

I still half-expect Robocop to arrive, but he never does. Let's just get this straight: I have walked into the heart of one of Britain's—and the world's—most surveilled-upon towns. I have peed into a litter bin—and I have damn well got away with it. Is this just beginner's luck?

I turn left into Abington Street, straight into another "CCTV radio watch area." Two shifty youths are loitering there. One of them approaches me, and I brace myself for a mugging. Will I lose my wallet, or will the youth run off after a blast from one of the talking lamp-posts? It turns out, thankfully, that he is a mugger of modest ambition. "Oi, you got 10 pence on you?" he asks. "No, sorry, I haven't," I say. "You f***ing pr**k!" he shouts as I hurry away. And still nothing from Jagger and Woody—or even a ticking-off from a five-year-old schoolchild.

Farther up the street, a gang of louts is hanging around, drunk. Two of them take a fancy to a potted tree, which has been planted to add a little country in the city. They grab it and haul it over, so that its broken trunk ends up at a 45-degree angle, with soil spilled over the pavement. "Come on Jagger, come on Woody," I want to scream, "Say something for Christ's sake!" But they don't. Next, I walk up to Sheep Street. There, underneath a sign reading "Still under surveillance—illegal dumping costs you" stands, er, a pile of discarded rubbish bags.

And so it went on: just a typical night out in an English town center. By the time I make my way through the labyrinth of soulless underpasses by the bus station and safely back to my car, I have spent two hours wandering around Northampton's town center, and not once do I hear so much as a recorded message from Jagger and Woody. But more to the point, neither, save for a few who briefly turn up to deal with a minor traffic accident, do I see a single police officer. This is one of Britain's "surveillance towns"— kitted-out, so I'm told, with a remote-control policing system—but it has virtually none of the real thing.

Northampton's CCTV system might catch you peeing in a litter bin, but more likely it won't. It is designed to give you the impression that everything you do in the town is under the gaze of some watchful law-enforcement officer—when the reality is that most of the screens spend most of their time unwatched. Northampton is a latter-day Panopticon: a prison designed by the nineteenth-century jurist and philosopher Jeremy Bentham to fool inmates into thinking that they were being constantly watched. The prison consisted of a central tower, whose windows, fitted with blinds, looked out

The last thing I would want is to be associated with the kind of pimply nerd who stays up all night in a wooden hut in the backwoods of Nebraska telling every chatroom in the world that the CIA has implanted a silicon chip in his brain. (Although it has to be said that this is now perfectly feasible. An American company, VeriChip, already markets a glass-encapsulated "radio-frequency identification device" that can be injected into human flesh, supposedly with the aim of speeding the passage of authorized people through security checks.) The truth is that I am not sure how much state surveillance is justified, how much is plain nosiness, and how much is actually dangerous. Should I be worried at the thought that MI5 might somewhere have a dusty file on me—or flattered?

All I do know is that mass surveillance of the citizenry is a subject which has undergone rather too little debate. Leaving the obvious nutters aside, it is hard to find a lot in the way of coherent discussion. Why is it that we feel so indifferent to the cameras on every street that are filming—and storing for many weeks—images of us going about our lives? Why do so few people rise in horror when a government minister—as Malcolm Wicks, the British science minister, did in April 2007—proposes that elderly people be fitted with satellite-tracking devices in case they get lost:

> We've got an ageing population, with many people frail and many suffering from dementia... How can we get the balance right so that these people have the freedom to live their lives, to go out into the community and go shopping, but also that some might benefit from being monitored so that their families know they are safe and secure?

Perhaps we are all so enthralled with celebrity culture that we are unable to see anything but benefit in being photographed and written about. It is notable that the expression "Big Brother," coined by George Orwell to describe the surveillance society, then—in the late 1940s—in its infancy, is now more associated with a TV reality show where volunteers allow themselves to be filmed for the entertainment of the television-watching public. Presumably, those who go on air do so in the belief that there is no such thing as bad exposure. In opening up their lives to the cameras they see career opportunities, easy fortunes. They don't see persecution and imprisonment, as the inhabitants of the surveillance societies of the former Soviet bloc saw every time they suspected themselves of being under observation.

Our own western surveillance societies, thankfully, cannot be compared with the autocracies of the old Eastern Europe, even if they borrow a few of their methods. But you might be shocked to find out just how much our government—potentially—knows about you. There is a term, a "data footprint," to describe the information that is gathered on each of us as we go about our daily lives. My quest was to discover just how big my "data footprint" has grown; not in a state of premeditated rage against an Orwellian state, but more in a spirit of discovery. I just wanted to find out what government agencies and private companies know about me—and what they do with the information.

What I found did not always strike me as sinister. As often as not, what struck me was how useless much everyday surveillance is. It seems to me that the more the authorities watch us, the less they seem able to see. We talk of a "surveillance society," sometimes of a "police state." But what kind of surveillance society is it that allows three terror suspects, held under a "control order"—which required them to report to the police every day, to wear electronic tags and to observe a curfew of 12 hours every day—to abscond, as Ibrahim Adam, Cerie Bullivant, and Lamine Adam did in May 2007, and apparently vanish off the face of the earth? Where was London's great barrage of CCTV cameras when the police were trying to track them down? Nowhere to be seen. It would be nice to think that they had been caught on camera slipping off down the High Street and onto a bus, and had left a trail of CCTV images leading to their lair, wherever it might be. But if they did show up on any CCTV cameras, the police are keeping jolly quiet about it.

They weren't the only ones who managed, unlike me on my trip to Southend, to give the surveillance society the slip. In 2003, it was reported that 416 tagged prisoners were on the run. They were supposed to be confined to their homes, the electronic tag setting off an alarm in the police station whenever it was taken outside the prisoner's wired-up home during proscribed hours. It didn't take the enterprising prisoners long, however, to work out the fatal weakness: they simply cut off their tags, left them at home (or in one case transferred them to their dog)—and ran away.

We imagine all this surveillance equipment to be omnipresent and hyper-observant, but frequently it has turned out to be completely ineffective. In other cases, the methods used by the surveillance society, while they might seem notionally sinister, are simply a reaction to technological developments. You cannot, to be blatant about it, police the internet by placing cops on the beat. You can only do so by means of electronic surveillance. But other things I found out did worry me. In fact, by the end of my quest I could hardly bear to use my computer for fear of setting off alarm bells in some government listening center.

I live in Britain, and therefore that is where I started: trying to find out what British organizations have gathered on me. But it quickly became obvious that the surveillance society does not respect national borders. I was soon to find out, for example, that details of my financial transactions are liable to end up whirring around the computers of a Belgium-based banking co-operative—where they may be picked up by the American CIA and analyzed for any links between myself and terrorist groups. More mundanely, the CIA also appears to know what airline meal I choose when I cross the Atlantic. The expression "global village" is usually taken to mean that the world has become a smaller place: many of us have friends on other continents with whom we can keep in regular contact, like medieval peasants around the village well. But the expression has come to take on another meaning: the global village has evolved into one of those villages where you cannot move without seeing twitching curtains, behind which lurk miserable old buggers intent on tracing your every step.

I don't have the largest data footprint in the world. I am not one of the 631 adults who were electronically tagged by the courts in 2004/05 to help keep them under control while they served community sentences (5,751 juveniles suffered the same fate). Neither am I one of the clubbers silly enough to take up the offer made by a chain of Spanish nightclubs in 2004—"allow us to implant a computer chip under your skin and we will allow you to bypass the queue." Neither, as far as I am aware, am I one of the 70 Americans who have been implanted with chips in order to help their carers find them if they wander off.

Theoretically, therefore, it should be an easy job finding out what the state knows about me. The Labour government of Tony Blair between 1997 and 2007 seemed enthusiastically to embrace greater openness in government. In 1998, the government updated the Data Protection Act to give us greater rights to discover what information is gathered on us. In 2005, Britain followed the US in adopting a Freedom of Information Act. Henceforth, in theory, any citizen would have the right to ask the government for information on any area of public administration. Information could still be withheld—clearly it would be absurd if the Act obliged the Ministry of Defense to disclose the position of army units on the battlefield—but government departments and agencies would have to give a good reason for withholding information. And not just because they felt like it or because it made life more convenient for them.

However, the government quickly struggled to live with the consequences of the Freedom of Information Act. Just 18 months after it came into operation it decided after all that it rather liked keeping its secrets. After 121,000 requests for information were made in 12 months it decided that it would try to limit requests, rationing individuals and organizations to two questions every 60 days. Some of the questions, ministers had complained, were frivolous—like the request to know how many windows there were in the Department for Work and Pensions HQ. Lord Falconer, however, had a slightly more revealing explanation: that too many requests were being made to calm "the wilder fevers of journalistic wish-lists." In other words, the government was a little worried we might actually find out something it didn't want us to know. One of those things was, er, the expenses of Members of Parliament. There soon followed a bill—which so far has failed to make it onto the statute book thanks to the efforts of MPs who favor openness—to exempt MPs from the Freedom of Information Act, so they can keep their earnings and expenses secret.

How very convenient that those who have appropriated our privacy should seek to protect their own. And how typical of the political elite.

But leave that aside for a moment, what about the surveillance society and me? What does the state know about my life, my travels and my habits, and in particular is there any other way it can tell that Wednesday, 16th May 2007, I made a trip to the end of Southend Pier?

CHAPTER THREE

Me and My Mug

"It was incredibly spooky because the face just didn't look human."

> — **Security guard at Hampton Court Palace**, interviewed after a "hooded ghost" was spotted on the building's CCTV system in December 2003.

The first year after CCTV cameras were installed in Baltimore, Maryland, in 2005, they helped police to solve not a single serious crime. "They're good for circumstantial evidence but it definitely isn't evidence we find useful to convict somebody of a crime," said State Attorney Office spokeswoman Margaret Burns. It fact, in many cases the CCTV footage had set police investigations on a false trail: on more than one occasion police had misidentified suspects thanks to grainy, blurred images.

So how much of my mug did those cameras on the end of Southend Pier really catch? As luck would have it, there was a way I could find out. Under the Data Protection Act of 1998 any citizen can demand, for a modest fee, to see certain data that is kept on him or her by public authorities. All I had to do was to write to customer services at Southend-on-Sea Borough Council, enclosing a check for £10, and I could have the image sent to me. Assuming my head wasn't a complete blob, I even had dreams of using the image on the cover of this book.

It seemed straightforward enough. I had been on the end of the pier at 4:25 p.m. on Wednesday 16th May, wearing a grubby blue raincoat. I was warned that the council could not supply photographs of anyone else except me, so I went to the trouble of emailing a photograph of myself to help them identify the right guy. The following week I received this response:

> Dear Mr. Clark,
>
> Thank you for returning the Council's standard form requesting CCTV footage together with a check for the £10 fee applicable.
>
> We do have video footage of a person that I believe could be yourself, however, all the cameras on the Pier Head at the time of the search were left showing a general view of the areas that they cover with the lens zoomed out, so that maximum coverage could be achieved. Had any suspicious behavior been noted, a camera could have been zoomed in to a level that a face could be recognized. As the subject was not behaving in a manner to attract the attention of an Operator, no such action was taken.
>
> As the footage we have is very general and a positive identification cannot be made, we cannot provide a copy of the footage for release under the Subject Data Access Request procedure, as the footage we have identified may not be of you.
>
> I have returned your check as we are unable to help you on this occasion.
>
> Yours sincerely,
> John Murphy
> Strategy & Policy
> ICT Division
> Southend-on-Sea Borough Council

But what if I had gone on to blow up the town hall? Wouldn't the police like to be able to survey the town's CCTV cameras for suspects, and be able to pick me out as I made my way around the town? Surely they would, and yet if they tried to trace my walk to the end of Southend Pier, all they would be able to see was a general view of the Thames Estuary. Now it becomes clear how three terror suspects, under control orders in the most enthusiastic surveillance society on Earth can simply vanish without trace. Big Brother is Watching: not you, but the lights twinkling in Sheerness.

Rather disappointed, I turned to the webcam on the end of the pier: surely I must have been caught on that—I would be able to print off a photo and at least have one souvenir from my day out in Southend. No such luck. It turned out that on the day I visited the webcam was broken.

The deficiencies of CCTV images have not stopped the cameras proliferating, especially in Britain, easily the most-watched nation on Earth. According to Camera Watch, a research body set up by the industry to improve the efficiency of CCTV stystems, there are now 4.2 million cameras in use in Britain, including those used in private surveillance systems. This equates to 1 for every 14 Britons. Theoretically, this should be sufficient for the entire nation to be photographed simultaneously, if anyone is minded to organize a record attempt for the *Guinness Book of Records*.

The CCTV society has crept up on us gradually over the past 40 years. The first CCTV camera was installed in Guy's Hospital, London in 1949 by the electronics company EMI. By the early 1970s they were widely installed in British shops, though they remained something of a novelty. If I behaved myself on shopping expeditions to Worcester in the early 1970 s, I was rewarded with a treat: I would be taken to Littlewoods, the department store, and allowed to perform in front of the closed circuit television camera that had just been installed at the front of the shop in order to deter shoplifters. In those days, the cameras were always combined with a television screen so that you could watch yourself. They were there to say: look, we can see you—put that sherbet back.

By the end of the 1970s, CCTV was making its first forays into public spaces. Britain did not lead the way at this stage, though it has been uniquely persistent in its devotion to CCTV over the following 30 years. Melbourne, Australia was an early enthusiast, installing its first camera in 1979. Yet in 2004, it voted to dismantle its network of 23 cameras on the grounds that they were not effective enough to justify the 500,000 Australian dollars in annual running costs.

An oft-quoted statistic has it that Londoners on average are caught on camera 300 times a day. The average Londoner must get out more than I do, but let's not quibble. There are a jolly large number of these things. In November 2006, the pressure group Privacy International produced a study comparing surveillance in 36 nations. In a measure of the extent to which states spy upon their citizens, Britain, thanks to its high number of CCTVs, tied for third place with Russia, lagging behind only China and Malaysia. Unlike Jeremy Bentham's jailer, they have not come cheap. The cameras have cost £500 million to install and, at one time in the 1990s, were consuming 78 percent of the Home Office's crime prevention budget. That is an immense investment, so what about the return?

There is plenty of debate on the sinister aspects of CCTV cameras; the specter of Big Brother and so on. Rather less is spoken on the fundamental issue of whether surveillance cameras are actually worth the money. An obvious questions looms: if CCTV cameras, and other forms of surveillance really work, surely Britain ought to be the safest country in the developed world, or at least the country with the fastest-plunging rate of crime and anti-social behavior. Yet the last International Crime Victims Survey, which consisted of interviews with 34,000 people in 17 countries in 2000, found rather the opposite: that 3.6 percent of Britons considered themselves to have been victims of crime in the previous 12 months—second only to Australia. Since then, the number of British CCTV cameras has continued to rise, as has violent crime and robbery—the very sort of crimes that tend to take place on the streets where CCTV cameras ought to act as a deterrent.

The presence of CCTV cameras hasn't done a great deal for Suresh Kumar, who runs a corner shop in Plaistow, East London. His premises have been raided 200 times over the past 10 years—an average of almost one attack a fortnight. And that is in spite of the CCTV camera installed inside his shop. The attackers must know the camera is there, but it seems to do little to deter them. Footage of one recent attack shows why: the fuzzy image of a figure in baseball cap and masked face, wielding a large stick, gives little away.

I am not alone in finding Northampton's network of 495 cameras, hugely expanded over the past five years, rather less than effective at fighting crime. Between 2002/03 and 2006/07, the number of violent crimes recorded by the Northamptonshire constabulary rose from 9,808 to 10,113, robbery from 1,015 to 1,037 and criminal damage from 15,688 to 16,025. Moreover, the clear-up rate declined: from 70 percent to 59.7 percent in the case of violent crimes, from 24.3 percent to 19.4 percent in the case of robbery, and from 16.8 percent to 13.5 percent in the case of criminal damage. There may, of course, be other reasons for this sorry picture, but it is hardly a ringing endorsement for a policing system based on CCTV cameras.

What about the drunken and anti-social behavior which has become a sad fixture in the center of almost all British towns: does the presence of CCTV cameras not do anything to curtail that? Not according to a four-year study in the late 1990s by the University Hospital Cardiff, which analyzed the experiences of five towns with CCTV cameras and five towns without. The presence of cameras was found to do nothing to detract from the willingness of citizens to engage in brawling and other forms of violence—even though those involved must have known that they were going to be caught on camera. The study suggested that CCTV cameras had proved useful in only one respect: in towns with CCTV cameras injuries from brawls were found to be less severe. The reason was that police were being called out a little quicker, and were able to break up fights a little sooner. But presumably the response would have been faster still had police been present on the streets in the first place.

In 2001, the Scottish Center for Criminology conducted a study into two CCTV schemes, in Airdrie and Glasgow. The latter scheme had been sold to the public on the promise that it would "eliminate" crime and increase the number of visitors by 225,000 a year. In Airdrie, crime fell by 21 percent during the first year following installation of the cameras, and the number of crimes solved increased by eight percent. In Glasgow, however, results were far less convincing. Crime fell slightly, but not as much as it had fallen in other towns and cities, which had not had cameras installed. The study also found that the cameras did little or nothing to improve residents' perception of the level of crime.

Many studies have reported an initial drop in crime following the installation of CCTV, followed by a return to normal when criminals become blasé about the cameras. Part of the reason they become blasé is that they quickly learn to evade supervision. In a 2003 study, Jerry Hart of the University of Leicester sought convicted shoplifters as volunteers, rigged them up with cameras and sent them into CCTV-monitored stores to attempt to recreate the offences for which they had earlier been convicted. He then studied how they went about their business—and how good the CCTV cameras were at picking them up. Although some admitted to having been caught by CCTV cameras before, none were caught in the experiment. Some relied on speed, reckoning that the response from a remote CCTV control room would be slow to catch them. As one of the volunteers noted, "I have never seen a CCTV camera jump off the wall and nick anyone." Others had managed to work out which parts of the stores were beyond reach of the cameras.

had failed to sound the alarm that a single one of the 25 faces in Newham's rogues' gallery was at large on the borough's streets.

Another trial of FaceIt—in Tampa, Florida in 2001 - did at least result in a number of alarms. Unfortunately, not one of the people picked out by the system turned out to be the person FaceIt thought he was. Fed up with pursuing harmless grannies who bore a passing resemblance to wanted serial killers, the police abandoned the trial after two months. Maybe facial recognition cameras will work one day, but for the moment I don't think I would be quaking in my boots if I were a wanted criminal roaming a town watched over by facial recognition software.

So much for CCTV's ability to deter criminals and to apprehend them. What about bringing them to justice? While there are certainly cases in which CCTV images have led to prosecution, the evidence suggests they are a poor substitute for human eyes and ears. In three-quarters of cases where police produce footage in court, the evidence is ruled inadmissible, usually because the images are so grainy they don't have a hope of identifying the culprit.

In sanctioning the use of CCTV the government has sometimes shown a keen awareness of privacy issues and the possibility that CCTV might lose public support if seen to be too much like Big Brother. But therein, too, lies part of the problem: the laws which are supposed to protect ordinary citizens from overbearing surveillance too often end up protecting the criminals the cameras are supposed to catch. A lot of CCTV footage ends up being dismissed as evidence in the courts because the operation of the camera failed to follow the many rules regarding its use. In 2007, Camera Watch, which advises councils and the police on CCTV systems, surveyed the nation's 4.2 million CCTV cameras and estimated that nine out of ten of them breach either the Data Protection Act or the Human Rights Act, making it easy for lawyers to challenge the use of footage as evidence. The law, for example, insists that all cameras be registered for a specific purpose such as "fighting crime," but in many cases, Camera Watch discovered, the systems were being used for purposes others than those for which they had been registered. You could, for example, successfully argue that footage of you hitting somebody over the head be ruled inadmissible in court if the camera which caught you doing the deed was only registered "for protecting property." Another common failing was a lack of security regarding the handling of images. The law insists that facial images of individuals be regarded in the same way as names and addresses—handled in a secure environment—yet many camera control rooms were situated where members of the public could see them.

One might easily regard these rules as petty—as indeed some of them are. Why, for example, do we need a law to protect our privacy from the possibility that our faces might be on view to anyone taking an idle peek into a shopping center's CCTV control room when anyone visiting the shopping center can see our faces in the flesh? It makes a nonsense of CCTV surveillance if anyone with a clever lawyer can simply have it dismissed in court.

On the other hand, it would make for poor law-enforcement if CCTV cameras were allowed to be used for any purpose at any time. To extrapolate from present trends, we would end up with an entirely remote-controlled police force, whose members reached their targets for solving crimes by trawling through endless CCTV footage to catch petty offenders. Britain has not—yet—reached the situation of Thailand, where a Swedish-born resident, Oliver Jufer, was jailed in March 2007 for 10 years for drunkenly spraying graffiti over a poster of His Majesty the King of Thailand (he could have got 75 years). But it is certainly the way things are going: among the soft targets recently pulled over for minor offences (thus helping the authorities reach targets for law enforcement) are 45-year-old Babiker Fadol, fined £50 and given a year's conditional discharge for putting his feet on the seats of a train in Liverpool, and a Kentish child arrested for throwing a cream bun at a bus. One wonders how much of a role CCTV cameras play in this trend towards the zealous prosecution of minor offenders and the less committed pursuit of career criminals. The existence of CCTV cameras is bound to skew law enforcement towards offences committed in public places, such as town center streets, and away from offences committed in dark alleys and private places not covered by CCTV. The fear that CCTV cameras simply displace crime from areas which are covered by cameras to areas which are not is a perfectly valid one.

So far, authorities have attempted to answer this question by installing more and more cameras. But where do you stop? Surely there are private places which not even Britain's Labour government would propose putting cameras. In March 2007, the Pakistan cricket coach and former England batsman Bob Woolmer was found dead in the bathroom of his hotel bedroom in Kingston, Jamaica a few hours after his team had been surprisingly eliminated from the cricket world cup. Given that Mr. Woolmer had told friends that he was minded to divulge information about illegal betting in the sport, there was an immediate suspicion of murder. As with most large modern hotels, CCTV was installed in the Pegasus Hotel: two cameras were trained on the lifts giving access to the floor where Mr. Woolmer was staying, and in theory they should have revealed who had visited his room. Much hope was placed in the footage, though in the event it proved to be fuzzy. And in any case it failed to cover the area where Mr. Woolmer died, in the bathroom of his room. Eventually, Jamaican police came to the conclusion that Mr. Woolmer had not been murdered at all but had died of a heart attack. Presumably, had CCTV been installed in the bathrooms of the hotel the exact circumstances of his death would have been clear from the outset—except that would be a violation of privacy which hardly anybody would advocate.

Or, maybe they would. Police have already experimented with installing CCTV in private homes. In 2002, West Midlands Police announced that they conducted a secret trial in Coventry which involved installing tiny infrared surveillance cameras in the homes of elderly people and frequent victims of burglaries (with the homeowners' permission) in order to catch burglars. The cameras, the size of a £1 coin, relayed images to a police station, and could be used as evidence in court. The trial, said the police, had been a great success: burglars, who had not been expecting surveillance cameras in Arthur and Doris's living room, proved easy meat. A number of serial offenders had been caught and crime had dropped accordingly.

It is hard to be too critical of this initiative. The cameras had been installed with the homeowners' consent and they were there for a specific purpose: to catch known offenders. And they did their job. But just one thing. If I were Arthur or Doris, I am not entirely sure that I would appreciate the local constabulary having an eye on my living room. Fine, if all you want to do is play dominos. But what if your home life is, shall we say, a little more exotic. Would you really want PC Bloggs, a pseudonymous police officer blogger, as an audience? There is also the question of legitimate visitors to Arthur and Doris's home. Ought they to be told that their visit will be on camera? When I wander into a shopping center, at least I receive some sort of warning in the shape of signs saying "CCTV in operation," so shouldn't I have that warning when Doris invites me round to tea and I start boasting about my illegal whisky distillery? Who would ever want to visit Arthur and Doris again?

The danger, as always with this sort of thing, lies in mission creep. It begins with an innovative way to catch a serial burglar in Coventry—but will it end in a situation where it is regarded as normal to have hidden cameras around your home wired up to the local police station, and, indeed, it might be come impossible for you to get a competitive insurance quote unless you consent to such devices.

If we are going to be persuaded to accept CCTV cameras into our homes and other private places, there arises an acute problem of trust. Not everyone who handles CCTV images has their mind entirely on the job. In 2005, a police officer at San Francisco's airport was suspended after being caught ogling female passengers on the airport's CCTV system. In July 2007, five CCTV operators at the Welsh Assembly building in Cardiff were fined after being caught training their cameras on the windows of private homes. While early CCTV cameras were very straightforward devices, modern ones, which allow the user to magnify parts of the image, provide huge opportunities for misuse.

The irony is that citizens using cameras in public are increasingly treated with suspicion. In one case in Surrey a couple innocently taking photographs in a public park were detained by members of a children's rugby club who suspected them of being pedophiles. The couple were later visited by the police who warned them that they must not take photographs of children. In 2007, Vale of Glamorgan Council attempted to place an outright ban on any member of the public taking photographs of children in its public parks. Ostensibly this was to guard against lurking pedophiles, but the ban also applied to parents taking photographs of their own—fully-clothed—children. Fortunately, on this occasion common sense prevailed, and the proposal was thrown out.

If private cameras in private hands are regarded with such suspicion by local authorities, why are they so relaxed about the misuse of CCTV images of our streets, parks, and swimming pools? The potential for misuse is clearly there. In a long-forgotten scandal in the early 1990s, a staff member at a gym used by the late Princess of Wales was arrested after installing a hidden camera in the ceiling above the machines on which she exercised.

Other CCTV images have mysteriously found their way onto the internet—or primetime television. In 2004, a sequence of a man shooting himself in the lobby of a block of flats in the US somehow turned up on a pornographic website— hardly reassuring for residents of housing developments covered by CCTV.

When CCTV cameras were first installed in British cities and main roads the government somehow forgot to explain that the police would be free to flog the footage to television stations, who have developed a lucrative genre of early evening entertainment: foolish motorists driving the wrong way down motorways and the like. This seems to be a worldwide phenomenon. Visit YouTube.com and you can feast your eyes all day on road accidents from Adelaide to Zharkent. I was astonished one day to be sent an email offering me the chance to view—for free—the latest road accidents in Guatemala.

To be fair, some steps have been taken to prevent the crass use of CCTV images—not least since 2003, when a suicidal Essex man attempted to slash his wrists on Brentwood High Street. An attentive CCTV operator spotted what was about to happen and dispatched a police van to the scene with the result that the man survived. Understandably pleased with their day's work, the police decided to release the images to the press and to television stations. Unhappily for the authorities, the would-be suicide was not so grateful for his 11th-hour rescue, and seized the opportunity to sue the authorities for breaching his right to a private life under the European Convention on Human Rights—a case he duly won (the images in this case being sufficiently clear that he was recognized by several friends).

Another individual to strike a blow against the misuse of surveillance cameras was Dr. John Diggle of Caerleon, South Wales, who in 2003 spotted a concealed camera on his property. Further enquiries revealed that it had been installed there by Gwent Police after his 14-year-old son had thrown an egg at a neighbor's car, the neighbor in question being a retired policeman with... Gwent Police. Dr. Diggle complained to the Police Complaints Authority which affirmed that the police do have the power to train secret surveillance cameras on your home for the purposes of tackling serious crime—although in this case there was considerable debate as to whether throwing an egg at a car fulfilled that criterion. At the Police Complaints Authority hearing it also transpired that Gwent Police had exceeded by three days the 28-day period in which they were allowed to operate the cameras. Dr. Diggle's complaints were upheld on a number of counts and he was awarded £50,000 in damages.

Somehow I suspect that he won't be the last to win a victory against the surveillance society. With cameras whirring on every street corner, the potential for a backlash against misuse of the images is huge. And it has hardly even begun.

CHAPTER FOUR

A Brief History
of Surveillance

1414 First record of passport being issued by King Henry V. Fortunately, he was able to find a way through customs for his own little trip to France.

1583 Sir Francis Walsingham, Queen Elizabeth's chief spymaster, gives birth to modern espionage by searching the home of Francis Throckmorton, then having him arrested and stretched on a rack to extract a "confession" to a plot to overthrown the Queen.

1841 French police establish the first "Rogues' Gallery" of crime suspects. Every prisoner is photographed so that his mug can be shown to witnesses of future crimes. The Governor of Bristol Gaol follows suit by establishing his own in 1854.

1861 Abraham Lincoln approves the tapping of telegraphs during the American Civil War.

1880 Dr. Henry Faulds, a British doctor working in Japan, publishes a paper in the scientific journal *Nature* describing how fingerprints left at the scene of a crime can be used to identify criminals.

1883 Alphonse Bertillon establishes the first database of human measurement. Having identified eleven different measurements, including the width of the head, the length of the right ear, and the distance from the left shoulder to the right middle finger, he proposes that records be used to identify suspects. Over the coming years, 100,000 individuals are subjected to what becomes known as "Bertillonage."

1889 German-American statistician Herman Hollerith invents a mechanical tabulating machine using punch cards to speed up the analysis of vast quantities of data. The following year it is used for the US Census, and the real business of counting people begins. An updated version is later used by Germany's Third Reich to sort its population into racial groups.

1908 Theodore Roosevelt asks Charles Bonaparte to form a body of investigators charged with fighting a growing crime wave. The result, the Bureau of Investigation, is renamed the FBI in 1935. Not to be outdone, the British government forms MI5 the following year.

1949 Electronics company EMI installs the first CCTV camera in Guy's Hospital, London. The current count of CCTV cameras in Britain is circa 4.2 million.

1958 Racing driver Maurice Gatsonides invents the first speed camera, with the aim of using it to help improve his driving around corners.

1972 The FBI installs the first fingerprint scanner.

1974 Britain establishes the Police National Computer, allowing forces to have instant access to the criminal records of all Britons.

1984 British scientist Sir Alec Jeffreys devises a test by which a person's identity can be confirmed by strands of his DNA.

1988 British passports become machine-readable for the first time. Out goes the concept of a stiff blue document demanding that Britons be allowed free passage around the world and in comes a floppy burgundy book whose main purpose is to help Customs and Excise maintain an electronic record of our every movement.

1992 The first "Gatso" speed camera is installed in Britain.

1995 The UK DNA database is set up. It is supposed to cover only serious criminals, but for some reason its scope rapidly expands.

2005 Bluewater Shopping Center in Kent bans youths wearing hooded sweatshirts, on the grounds that they are not showing enough of their faces to be identified on a CCTV image.

CHAPTER FIVE

ME AND MY GENES

*"A great many people who are walking the streets,
and whose DNA would show them guilty of
crimes, go free."*

> — **Lord Justice Sedley**, advocating that DNA samples from every man,
> woman, and child in Britain be added to the National DNA Register.

It was too late before I realized what I had done. Unthinkingly I had gripped the metal handrail to Southend Pier, thereby leaving a record of my visit which would last several months. It was only when I got home that I realized this—after reading the story of an elderly anti-nuclear protester from Hamburg, Germany who, early in 2007, was awoken at 8 a.m. by a knock on the door. He opened up to find the police on his doorstep with an unusual request: that he clench a metal bar which they had brought with them. They then took away the bar. From it was taken an odor sample which was then stored in a library of sweat samples, to be used for the policing operation at the G8 summit in Heiligendamm in June. Should the protestor attempt to penetrate the eight-mile-long barbed wire fence that had been erected around the Baltic resort, the police dogs would be easily able to sniff him out.

This is not a novel policing technique. The German police learned it from the Stasi, the hated secret police force of East Germany. That is not to say that the actions of the German police in this case compared with their counterparts behind the Iron Curtain. Anti-globalization protest groups made no secret of their intentions to blockade the G8 summit and to beat up policemen—indeed they broadcast them on the internet. But the story does show how methods once associated only with malign dictatorships have become part of policing in democratic nations. Moreover, it shows how easily we drip our DNA behind us wherever we go.

That each of us has a unique DNA "fingerprint" (save for identical twins) has been known since the 1940s. It wasn't until the 1980s, however, that a team led by British scientist Professor Sir Alec Jeffreys devised a means of utilizing DNA for identification. The method consists of analyzing ten parts of a long strand of DNA—genetic information which is particular to each individual and which can be derived from a single hair or bead of sweat. This DNA profile can then be used to link a criminal suspect to genetic material—say from blood, sweat, or hair—found at the scene of a crime: a process known as DNA profiling. The chances of two people sharing the same DNA signature—again with the exception of identical twins—is said to be one in a billion, assuming, that is, that there is no contamination and the DNA information is complete.

From this discovery was born, in 1995, Britain's National DNA database. As far as I know, I am not yet on this database—unless someone has swabbed me in my sleep without my noticing. But how much longer I can keep off it is another question. When set up, the database was supposed to be for known criminals only. However, by 2007, 3.7 million Britons—six percent of the population—had found their way onto it. Among them were 883,888 children, 100 of them under 10, including a pair of girls picked up by the local constabulary for the heinous crime of drawing on the pavement in chalk. Not everyone on the DNA database has even risen to this level of wrongdoing. In practice the police have added records of everyone they have arrested or in many cases simply called in for questioning. And the scope is widening all the time. In 2007, the government announced plans to relax the rules so that police will have the right to take DNA samples from citizens charged with minor offences, such as littering or failing to wear a seatbelt. Not only that, in the future the government wants the police to be able to take DNA samples in the street, using mouth swabs, greatly increasing the opportunities for getting people onto the database.

DNA profiling has proved a useful tool in providing evidence to link known suspects to the scene of a crime. Let's say you are a police detective who has a suspect, and evidence to link him with the crime. It works like this: you take a sample of his DNA, compare it with material found on the suspected murder weapon, and thus either confirm your suspicions or not. In these cases, the DNA evidence backs up other evidence, effectively removing any lingering doubt that the suspect was at the scene. Had DNA testing been around in the early 1960s, for example, it would have silenced those who protested the innocence of James Hanratty, hanged for the "A6" murder, in which a government scientist was killed and his lover injured while enjoying each other's company in a Morris Minor parked in a layby outside Bedford. In 2002, DNA evidence established beyond doubt that Hanratty was the killer.

It is a very different matter, however, now that police have started to trawl through the DNA database looking for matches—effectively treating 3.7 million people as potential suspects. The technique has already been used to jail—among others—Antoni Imiela, who in 2004 received seven life sentences for a string of sex attacks on women and girls around the M25 highway. He was already on the DNA database for having previously been jailed for armed robbery, and he was arrested for the sex attacks after his DNA was found to match material found at the scene of the first attack.

In Imiela's case, there was plenty of evidence to leave few in doubt of his guilt, but what if the National DNA database discovers a match with somebody for whom there is no circumstantial evidence to link him or her with a crime? Should that be considered to be conclusive evidence that the person is guilty? Some would like to think so. It is often repeated, not least in court, that the theoretical chance of achieving a false positive in a DNA test is just one in a billion—a jolly big number which would convince most juries of the accuracy of DNA profiling.

But even if this theoretical rate of accuracy really does reflect the genuine chances of achieving a false match—which is difficult to prove given that no DNA database yet has a billion people in it—would it be sufficient? Sir Alec Jeffreys doesn't think so: he has warned that, now the police are using the DNA database to fish for suspects, a more stringent form of DNA record should be devised, one which records a greater number of parts of a strand of DNA. A risk of one in a billion of finding a false positive may sound impressively low, but if the database comes to cover the entire British population of 60 million people it would mean that a search through the data for someone whose DNA matched that at the scene of a crime would have a 1 in 16 chance of picking out an entirely innocent person.

It isn't just the number of Britons on the DNA database that must be considered. In March 2007, the European Union revealed plans for a massive database of fingerprints covering the entire population of the EU's 27 member states: 493 million people. Trawling a database of this size for positive matches with material found at the scene of the crime would be certain to result in innocent people being jailed. You can just imagine the situation. There is a murder in Berlin. DNA data is relayed to police in all EU member states. Somewhere out there, whether it be a waiter in Portugal, a sheepherder in Greece or an oil worker in Aberdeen, there is a 50-50 chance of finding a match. In court the prosecution makes the case: "There is only a one in a billion chance that this information could be wrong." How many juries, presented with such information, would not convict?

There is another point to make here. By putting too much faith in the DNA database the police may end up encouraging criminals to plant false DNA trails. What havoc one might cause by embarking on burglary missions with a stolen pair of gloves and a secondhand coat—which, when the police searched through the DNA database for a match, would implicate innocent people.

One doesn't want to exaggerate the threat to innocent citizens from DNA profiling, nor present it as some kind of sinister process which is jailing innocent people by the dozen. But when was there debate over the decision to extend the DNA database by stealth to encompass 3.7 million Britons, a number which is growing at 500,000 people a year? Er, it wasn't. From the initial, limited plan to keep a database of known offenders, DNA profiling has gained a momentum which has proved hard to stop. No prizes for guessing what will come next: once the majority of Britons have, by stealth, been added, it will become a "tidying-up" exercise to do as Lord Justice Sedley suggested in September 2007, and add the rest of us.

The rest of us, that is—with one exception. As far as I can make out there is only one way to ensure that you keep off the DNA database: become a terrorist. While the DNA database now contains children caught playing hopscotch in the street, it does not contain any terror suspects on control orders—a watered-down form of house arrest in which the suspect has to report regularly to police. In June 2007, Home Secretary John Reid made the startling admission that the 2005 Prevention of Terrorism Act has been drafted in such a way as to prevent the police from taking fingerprints and DNA samples from terror suspects issued with control orders. In other words, the one group of people not represented on the database is precisely the group you would most want to be on it.

There is also the question of what is, and might in future, be done with the information on the DNA database. Anyone who imagines that DNA data is being used purely for its stated purpose—to solve crime—is being cruelly misled. In 2006, the *Observer* newspaper reported that the Home Office had given approval for DNA data to be used in 20 medical studies, the aim of which is to establish whether or not there is a genetic link to criminality. In other words if you find yourself on the DNA register your genes will be analyzed to see whether they are shared by others who have been arrested for similar offences. Presumably, once these studies have finished their work, we will be able to test the DNA of babies as soon as they emerge from their mothers' wombs. If they are found to be constructed from a genetic make-up similar to that of known criminals, they can then safely be incarcerated for life.

In reality, of course, it won't be as blatant as that: more likely, the information that a baby possesses criminal genes will be passed on to social workers, who can then devise a "care plan" to monitor their development, perhaps involving seizure from their natural parents at an early age. But either way, people with "criminal genes" will be considered guilty from birth.

It would be comforting to think that this is still in the realm of science fiction. Yet in November 2006 the Metropolitan Police's Homicide Prevention Unit admitted to building a database of 100 people whom it believes are likely to commit rape or murder. Using information gleaned from interviews with social workers, medical staff, and, in cases where domestic violence has been reported, statements from family members, the suspects—or potential suspects—are then subjected to "criminal profiling": the science that studies patterns of offending. Those who show up as a high risk can then be targeted with surveillance, and persuaded, where appropriate, to seek medical attention.

Is that unreasonable, to predict serious crime with the aim of preventing it? Few people, I suspect, would say that it was—so long as, that is, their own name had not somehow found its way onto the future criminals' database. The question is, once you have established the principle of "convicting" people of crimes you think they will commit, where do you stop? Are people to be banned from driving on the basis that they show aggression on the go-kart track as children? Do you ban someone from working on tills because his habit of telling lies as a child fits a pattern that suggests he will grow up to be a fraudster?

Well yes, actually. It is an uncomfortable reality that no matter how ridiculous the scenarios one imagines, sooner or later they will become a reality. A few days after I conceived of the above possibilities, the government announced a review of the use of surveillance in crime-fighting, the aim of which would be to target "the offender and not the crime." One of the suggestions was to identify from an early age children who fitted the profile of a serial offender later in life. Such children would be put on a database and have their progress at school and at home monitored by social workers.

The outcome of this novel approach to tackling crime, needless to say, is only as good as the science behind it. And that, at present, is sorely untested. Moreover, by labeling children as potential criminals from an early age might we not just be encouraging them to misbehave? I have never made a habit of petty vandalism, but I have a feeling that were I to get wind of the fact that social services had marked me out as a danger to the public, I might just go and throw a brick through their window.

The direction of much of the current work with DNA sounds ominously like the work of US anthropologist William Sheldon, who from the 1940s through the 1960s photographed 20,000 naked Ivy League students from three angles—under the guise of studying their posture—in order to further his theory that a person's physical form and their mental and moral traits were linked. At the simplest level, Sheldon used detailed measurements taken from the photographs to classify the students into one of three "somatotypes": Endomorphics (fat, relaxed, and jolly people), Mesomorphics (muscular, courageous, and assertive people) and Ectomorphics (thin, fragile, artistic, and introverted people). At a more complex level, each individual was assigned a three digit code that, Sheldon believed, could be used to predict future achievement—and future criminal behavior.

Sheldon's work is now discredited, and most, though far from all, of the photographs have been shredded. But remarkably it took until the 1970s for the work to be dismissed as bunk. What about those 20,000 students, which included Hillary Clinton and former President George H. W. Bush: didn't it occur to them that there was something just a little bit odd, upon entrance to university, about being asked to report to a darkened room to be snapped in the buff? Where was the famed rebelliousness of student life, then? A generation that savagely denunciated its politicians was somewhat more pliant, it seems, when it came to agreeing to do what the men in white coats told them. It is easy to jump on Sheldon now, but I wouldn't mind betting that in 30 years' time we will be going through exactly the same sort of scandal again—this time involving theories derived from the British DNA database.

The existence of the DNA database is not exactly helping the government in its aim of eradicating "institutional racism" in the police and justice system: while 22 percent of young white males have found their way onto the database, 77 percent of young black males have had their DNA put on record. One has a horrible feeling, too, that this discrepancy may be used in order to justify putting everyone on the DNA database.

Inadvertently discriminating against minorities is something of a hazard for authorities who monitor the population. There is a precedent for a database which sets out with one purpose, and ends up achieving what looks like another: in 1927, Canadian authorities set up the Liquor Control Board of Ontario, charged with the duty of constructing a "drunk list" of individuals who could not be trusted with alcohol, and whom the Board's shops would not serve. The drunk list, which also included details of racial origin and social status, quickly evolved into what become dubbed the "Indian list." It had an uncanny habit of classifying most native Americans as drunks, while white middle-class tipplers escaped such a classification.

Nor is it just race which is bound to creep into DNA analysis. An evolving area of forensic science is lifestyle-profiling. A team from King's College, London has found a way of analyzing fingerprints for traces of nicotine—indicating that the person who left the prints is a smoker. Moreover, they believe that they can analyze fingerprints for traces of other chemicals that would indicate the consumption of certain foods and drinks. With this, they believe, it will be possible to build a profile of a suspect, notably his diet. This information might, just possibly, lead to the arrest and conviction of an offender. Equally, it might just be used, say, to decide whether or not an individual should qualify for healthcare on the NHS, or whether he should be offered a job. Do we really want a world in which we are continually asked for samples of our sweat whenever we access public services, so that it can be analyzed for clues as to our lifestyle habits?

No wonder science fiction has gone a bit out of fashion: it is becoming hard to imagine any scenario connected with the surveillance society that some geek in a government department or private surveillance company is not already turning into reality. But how about this one: what if the database of fingerprints collected from the scenes of crime ends up being hooked up with the database of your supermarket loyalty card—which holds all the relevant information on your shopping habits? Sweat left behind at a crime scene suggests that the culprit has a weakness for doughnuts and Jack Daniels. A computer hurriedly searches through records of millions of shoppers and picks out a few likely suspects—including you. So, you wake up one morning to find the police surrounding your house. You have become an innocent victim of lifestyle-profiling.

As yet—I think—this remains science fiction. But it provides one more reason, perhaps, to turn down the offer of a supermarket loyalty card.

No one should be fooled into thinking that in volunteering information about themselves to private companies, it will not be shared with public law-enforcement agencies. Indeed, in the US the state has come to rely heavily on information gathered by the private sector. Privacy laws frequently prevent public agencies gathering information about citizens, but they leave a loophole: They do nothing to prevent those agencies simply buying the information from the private sector. The result: the surveillance state has effectively been contracted out.

So would you volunteer your DNA to a private company, knowing that it could one day be used by the state as evidence against you? Two people who think you should are Linda Avey and Anne Wojcicki, who between them have set up a company, 23andMe, which aims to collect millions of samples of DNA from willing members of the public for use in tracing relatives, marketing, medical diagnostics, and, as much as one can glean from the company's rather ethereal prospectus, dating. Collecting DNA samples will become just like collecting signatures to be read by graphologists.

The company has convinced Google sufficiently of the possibilities of private DNA gathering for the search engine to invest in it to the tune of $3.9 million. "Our goal is to connect you to the 23 paired volumes of your own genetic blueprint (plus your mitochondrial DNA)," reads the company's mission statement, "bringing you personal insight into ancestry, genealogy, and inherited traits. By connecting you to others we can also help put your genome into the larger context of human commonality and diversity."

I am guessing that to at least three-quarters of those who might chance upon 23andMe's website the above words mean absolutely nothing at all. For most of the other quarter there might be just a flicker of understanding what the company is trying to do. Yes, it wants you to give a sample of your DNA, which it will keep in a private library. It will then use the information to put you in touch with long-lost relatives around the world and write your own life horoscope, based on your inherited traits—effectively putting to recreational use the methods that the government is employing to fight crime. How, exactly, it plans to break the news to you when it discovers you have a genetic tendency to develop pancreatic cancer in your late 40s, the company does not quite say.

As for the putting your genome into the "human commonality and diversity" bit, I love it. If I have got it correctly, 23andMe wants to get hold of your DNA so it can rummage through its DNA library and say: "You are a blonde-haired, blue-eyed man with a shy, introverted nature, and boy, have we found the ideal complement to you—a dark-haired outgoing Polynesian." How endearingly diverse. More disturbingly, I can see a DNA library being of equal use to the local secretary of the Ku Klux Klan who wants to target bulk mail at the right sort of people. One can extrapolate from the company's mission statement to work out a few other possibilities: presumably, the technology will evolve to the stage at which certain genetic types can be associated with certain buying patterns—at which point your DNA will mark you out for a bombardment of genetically-targeted marketing material.

23andMe does not say that it won't hand your DNA sample over to the cops. In fact it says it will—although only under proper legal order. Anyone interested in sending in a sample of spit, knowing that it could lead to the cops nailing you for a crime committed in Alabama thirty years ago? It wouldn't surprise me if millions hand over their DNA without even stopping to consider these possibilities—such is our deferential attitude towards all things technological.

One thing is for sure: if 23andMe and Google are right in their judgment that millions of computer-users will be happy to spew their DNA around the world, it will soften public resistance to DNA registers encompassing the entire population.

CHAPTER SIX

ME AND MY GOOD NAME

"This document does not constitute a certificate of good character."

> — Letter in response to my enquiry as to whether I appear
> on Britain's Police National Computer.

For those who flippantly describe Britain as a "police state," an admission by the Home Office in 2007 must have come as something of a shock: Britain's police forces, it was revealed, have lost contact with 322 registered sex offenders. How can it be that a "surveillance society" with 4.2 million CCTV cameras, numerous number plate recognition cameras, and a growing DNA database can simply lose contact with over three hundred convicted rapists, child molesters, and child-pornography merchants who are supposed to be under close supervision?

The glib answer, as so often is the case when public services are criticized, is "lack of resources." If only we had more officers and case workers, said police forces in response, we could better keep an eye on all these flashers and gropers. As it is, it turns out that "supervision" of sex offenders can amount to as little as one visit from a probation officer a year. Too bad if the offender has fled in the meantime without leaving a forwarding address.

The question is, just how many case workers would it take to keep an eye on the 29,973 people who have already been added to Britain's sex offenders' register—not to mention the 14,317 violent offenders who are also supposed to be under supervision? With the country's prisons bursting—the jail population broke through the 80,000 mark in 2007, prompting a mass release of prisoners to create more space—the monitoring of offenders outside jail has become an ever more-important part of crime prevention. The existence of offenders' registers—technically known as Multi-Agency Public Protection Arrangements (MAPPA)—gives the impression that everything is under control, that people perceived as being a risk to the public can't so much as unzip their flies without a police officer pouncing upon them. Yet the supervision of offenders in the community is largely an illusion: it consists of personal details being added to a large database, the occasional visit from a social worker, and the ritual rounding-up of local offenders for questioning when a crime has been committed. What it isn't is what many members of the public perhaps imagine it to be, and how the former Home Secretary David Blunkett described it: "A prison without bars." Monitoring offenders in the community via surveillance methods hasn't proved a great success. In 2003/04, 6,415 convicted criminals released early from jail had to be sent back inside after re-offending. And those, of course, are just the ones who get caught.

As a study of MAPPA by de Montfort University, Leicester discovered, too often individuals on the sex offenders' register can throw the system into confusion by moving from one area of the country to another—even assuming that the offender has co-operated and informed the police of his change of address. Several police forces were so disillusioned by the ability of sex offenders to disappear that they had threatened to sub-contract the monitoring of offenders to the general public—by releasing the offenders' details to the press.

Matters are certainly not being made easier by the explosion in the number of people on the sex offenders' register, caused by the ever-increasing number of offences being classified under this definition. When set up by the Sex Offenders Act 1997, the register was intended to include only those convicted of rape or other serious sexual offences, usually on their release from prison. Those on the list have to register their address with the local police force. The police are then charged with the duty of assessing the risk posed by each individual and coming up with a management plan for them, which might consist of such things as housing the offender in supervised accommodation, electronic tagging, or "victim empathy work." But you can get on the register nowadays by any act that "outrages public decency"—which could well be construed to include any tarty blonde showing a bit of bum cleavage. In fact, to judge by town centers on a Friday night half of British youth would seem to qualify for inclusion.

Sex offenders are not the only ones to have found that escaping from Britain's "prison without bars" is a good deal easier than getting out of the real thing. No need to have a hacksaw blade smuggled in with the wife's cake; muggers and thieves fitted with satellite-monitored tags have simply carried on thieving and attacking—correctly calculating that there are not enough people monitoring their movements. One in four prisoners released from jail early so that they could be put on the electronic tagging scheme between 2004 and 2006 reoffended while supposedly under constant surveillance. One was missing for more than six months. Some had worked out that the equipment did not function properly in narrow streets with tall buildings—ideal mugging territory, in other words.

If authorities cannot successfully monitor the movements of several thousand prisoners fitted with electronic tags, what hope have they of keeping an eye on the many thousands more on various offenders' registers? Britain's "police state" is a virtual one: in theory, criminals are under constant supervision. In reality, once the bureaucracy of managing the databases has been undertaken there are too few police left to engage in any genuine surveillance.

The sex offenders' register hasn't exactly done a huge amount to stem sex offences, which have nearly doubled to 62,081 in the 10 years since the register was set up. There has been a simultaneous fall in conviction rates: 30 years ago a third of reported rapes ended with a conviction; by 2003/04 that was down to just six percent. It is possible that more offences are being reported because more efforts are being made to persuade victims to report offences. But even so, one wonders whether the police are simply being swamped with data and so burdened with the duty of preparing monitoring plans that they are neglecting more traditional police work, such as having a few police on the streets and solving crimes.

Our national fetish for databases does not end with the sex offenders' register. I am not sure exactly how many official databases there are in the UK: due to a remarkable oversight the government has yet to instigate a central database of databases. But it must run into hundreds at least. Some, like the Driver and Vehicle Licensing Authority's register of all vehicles in Britain, have existed for decades. Others, such as the sex offenders' register, have grown in recent times out of databases which have been around a long time—in this case "List 99," a database of sex offenders banned from teaching in schools.

The queen of British databases is the Police National Computer, a database of criminals established in 1974 and maintained by the Association of Chief Police Officers (ACPO). Seven million Britons have found their way onto this register, either by being convicted of a crime, being arrested, or merely for being cautioned. And once on it, you are on it for life. In some ways this is reasonable enough: if you break into a bank, shouldn't the police officers who pick you up loitering outside a jewelers 40 years later at least have access to the information of your earlier conviction?

The trouble is—as with any database of this size—while it gives the impression of being an infallible record of all criminal activity, in practice it is strewn with errors. According to a report by the Police Inspectorate, 22 percent of records entered onto the Police National Computer by police forces contained an error—in spite of having been checked by a supervisor. As a result, 2,700 people have been wrongly connected with criminal activity, with the result that some have been turned down for jobs.

Should you find yourself on the database, you will certainly face an uphill struggle being deleted from it. According to ACPO, names may be removed from the Police National Computer only in "exceptional circumstances." Asked to elaborate, ACPO told me of the case of a student who had been found dead in his digs. All others who lived in the building were arrested, fingerprinted, and questioned. Only it then turned out that that the dead student had in fact died of natural causes. Given that no crime had been committed, ACPO did on that occasion graciously agree to remove the names of the other students, so that they did not have to endure a lifetime of being tagged as murder suspects.

So how do you find out whether you are on the Police National Computer? There is a way: you send off a form to your local constabulary, along with a £10 note, and ask that they undertake a "Subject Access Data Request" under the Data Protection Act. When I did this, I wasn't sure whether to be relieved or a little disappointed when the answer came back negative. Just one word of warning if you are thinking of doing the same: the form does invite you to make an inadvertent confession by asking whether there is any reason you suspect that you might be on the Police National Computer.

One database which I won't escape from—or at least my children won't—is the government's planned £241 million Children's Index. This monster will carry health, education, and social service records on each of the nation's 15 million children, and will be made available to 330,000 doctors, social workers, and other state functionaries. The idea is that any of these professional groups will be able to enter a warning "flag" against a child's record because, say, he has been brought to a surgery with an injury, is overweight, or has been under-performing at school. Once a child has two warning flags a welfare investigation will follow. Any of the 330,000 authorized users will be able to access private data on children from any computer—though the guidelines do helpfully suggest that it wouldn't be a good idea for users to access the information while in an internet café, in case they forget to log off when they have finished and allow the names, addresses, medical records, exam results, and any social worker reports to be seen by the general public.

The government defends its children's database by saying that it will prevent another case like that of Victoria Climbie, the eight-year-old girl who died at the hands of her aunt and partner in 2000, after social workers failed to take action on signs of violence and abuse. But how? Social workers in the Climbie case were faxed details of Victoria's injuries from the hospital where she had been treated, but failed to read the fax properly. As one critic of the database memorably put it in response to a consultation exercise: "When you are looking for needles, why is it necessary to keep constructing haystacks?"

A separate database is planned for the 9.5 million people who work with children or who come into contact with them via clubs, or simply because they help with reading at their children's school. Under the Safeguarding Vulnerable Groups Act 2006, anyone who comes into contact with children through work or leisure activities will have to submit themselves for vetting, even if that contact is limited to parents helping out with reading in their children's class. Will it help tackle child abuse? It will certainly help create more criminals: failure to register will be a criminal offense subject to a fine of up to £5,000.

It is easy to imagine this great quest for databases leading to a society in which all our movements and all our actions are faultlessly logged, and in which the information is used against us when we apply for a job or a visa in years to come. But that is hopelessly to overestimate databases. A small database, say of several hundred offenders, can be of great use. It is relatively easy to keep the information up to date, and to process it when it needs to be processed. But one with several million names on it? How do you process the information then, and ensure that the records are accurate? There is a fundamental rule about databases: the bigger they are, the more useless they become.

This became obvious to the Paris police soon after they set up a "rogues' gallery" of the city's worst-known offenders in 1841. When there were a few names on it, officers trying to solve crimes found it easy to flick through the records, but when every common thief was added, it became a fog of information impossible to penetrate. It should have been obvious to the Derbyshire Constabulary, too, which in 2007 decided to send out letters to residents in the Derby suburb of Peartree offering them an amnesty if they admitted to past offences, so that they could make a fresh start. One of the letters found its way to a six-year-old boy. At least no one can say the police are not being thorough.

And next? In June 2007, the then Home Secretary John Reid proposed a national terrorists' register: a one-stop shop for any authority which needs to know whether the slightly shifty-looking caretaker it is just about to appoint to look after the town hall is a convicted terrorist likely to blow the place up. The register will include not merely those caught trying to light a fuse leading to a gunpowder barrel, but anyone convicted of belonging to a proscribed organization. As with the sex offenders' register, any citizen who finds himself on the terrorists' register will have to report to police if he changes address, goes on holiday, or spends more than five days away from home.

I have some doubts about this register. After all, what are we paying our security services for if not to monitor the movements of terrorists? One presumes that they have a database of dodgy individuals whom they keep an eye on. It would be a tiny bit late once they have blown up a London bus to discover that they have been missing from their home for six days.

The worry I have is that this is part of a campaign by stealth eventually to get us all on a register of some sort. It is terrorists and sex offenders today—fair enough—but, following the experience of the National DNA register, I would not be at all surprised if tomorrow we did not end up with a National Tax-Dodgers' Register, a National Speeders' Register and a National Litter-Droppers' Register—forcing almost all of us, for one reason or another, to declare our movements to the police.

Maybe we will all end up being electronically tagged. In June 2007, John Hutton, the Work and Pensions Secretary, floated a new idea for dealing with absent fathers who fail to pay maintenance for their children. In future, he suggested, they could be electronically tagged. I can see the rationale behind freezing their bank accounts, but fixing them with electronic tags? Why do they need to be followed around wherever they go? Is the state keeping an eye on them to make sure they aren't out conceiving more children? One comes to the conclusion that tagging, far from achieving any useful purpose, is simply being developed as a form of cruel and unusual punishment.

CHAPTER SEVEN

ME AND MY SECRETS

"Bruv, you don't think this place is bugged,
do you?"
"No. Do you know, I think we give them too
much credit, bruv."

> — **Islamic terrorist Omar Khyam and a co-plotter** discuss the
> competence of MI5, shortly before being arrested. They were, in fact,
> being bugged, and were later jailed for conspiring to cause explosions.

Just occasionally, one wishes that the British state would be a little more underhand in the way it spies on its people. On April 30, 2007, Omar Khyam and four of his associates were jailed for life for plotting to blow up Londoners with the aid of 600 kg of ammonium nitrate, which Omar had stashed away in a self-storage warehouse in West London. The conviction, not to mention the prevention of a terrorist atrocity, was thanks to some pretty sterling work by MI5, Britain's internal security service. Several times Omar had lovingly gone to inspect his cargo—seemingly unaware that MI5 was photographing him doing so and had taken the precaution of substituting the fertilizer with an inert substance.

But why, given the sheer number of petty security measures which have been pushed through in the name of defending us against Islamic terrorists over the past few years (such as confiscating nail files at airport security), are prosecutors still forbidden from using evidence gained from telephone taps in court? Fortunately, enough bugs were planted around Omar

Khyam's home (evidence from which is allowed to be used in court) to secure a conviction. But the fact remains: had the only incriminating evidence against him and his co-plotters been obtained via telephone taps, he would still be a free man.

This is one of the absurdities of the surveillance society. The general population is routinely subjected to surveillance, with little regard to privacy. And yet when the secret services latch on to a genuine security threat, they are obliged to behave in accordance with some bizarre gentlemanly code. Telephone taps in court, what? Good gracious, no. Terribly unsporting, old chum.

At least the government finally came round, in June 2007, to wondering whether it might be a good idea after all to allow phone tap evidence to be used in court. The matter is currently under review. But one's faith in the ability of Britain's surveillance czars to distinguish between the threats posed by terrorists and petty tax dodgers is not enhanced by the revelation that in the process of monitoring the activities of Omar Khyam, MI5 also came across one of his associates, a Yorkshire teaching assistant by the name of Mohammed Sidique Khan. After listening in on him for a while, the security services asked the police to carry on with the job. The police failed to do so—with the result that Khan was allowed, with three other plotters, to explode three bombs on the London Underground and one on a London bus on July 7, 2005, killing 52 people.

The only comfort we can take from the security service's failure to monitor the July 7th bombers is that it seems improbable, given that a lack of resources prevented Mohammed Sidique Khan being allocated a tail, that MI5 is spying on ordinary citizens in the way that the secret services of the Soviet bloc used to. Not that a lack of resources has restrained its instinct for file-gathering: it now has files on 272,000 British citizens—1 in 220 of the population. I was almost flattered, when I read this figure, to think that I might be considered sufficiently interesting to be among them.

So what kind of organization is MI5 and, more to the point, is it really spying on me?

In 1992, then-Prime Minister John Major stood up before MPs in the House of Commons to make a solemn announcement: that MI5 actually existed. He then went on announce that Christmas that year would be held on December 25th and that evidence had emerged that the Pope was a follower of Catholicism. As almost everybody was aware, MI5 had existed since 1909. Indeed, the only surprise that day was for the neighbors of Stella Rimington in Islington, North London, who that day was revealed to be head of the hitherto secret organization. She was a very nice neighbor, they told reporters, except that they had believed she worked for Marks and Spencer.

MI5 has come a long way since its emergence from the shadows. It now has a website and openly recruits for its staff through newspaper adverts, rather than, according to legend, at shady Oxbridge sherry parties—although the reality was always less glamorous: a friend of mine was approached after he turned up at the Cambridge University career center at a complete loss with what to do with his life. The careers officer reeled off a range of possibilities—accountancy, sales, marketing—at all of which my friend miserably shook his head. As a last resort the careers officer visited a dusty filing cabinet, withdrew a form and said: "Well, there is always the security services."

The most dramatic change of all is that MI5 is now, theoretically at least, supposed to tell you whether it keeps a file on you, and, if so, to give you an idea of the contents. This freedom was won as a result of a case brought in the High Court by the Liberal Democrat MP Norman Baker, which proved that MI5 does not have a blanket exemption under the Data Protection Act. As a result of his efforts, Mr. Baker discovered that MI5 had a file on him—a consequence, he believes, of his activities as an environmental protester. He further forced MI5 to reveal that it keeps files on 272,000 other adults.

You, too—theoretically—can see whether you are interesting enough to be among those 272,000 people. What you have to do is write to the Enquiries Desk, PO Box 3255, London SW1P 1AE, and make a "subject access request" under the Data Protection Act of 1998.

Reader, I couldn't resist. I wrote off and a few days later received a nice letter, on rather fetching MI5-headed notepaper (though lacking an address), asking me to fill in the attached form and send it back with a check for £10. I had got halfway through the form before I began to question the wisdom of what I was doing. Could I please fill in my address details—for everywhere I had lived since birth—and tell them whether there was any particular incident in my life that I suspected might have given rise to my having aroused the security services? Well, er, ought I really to mention the time I ended up in bed with the tart who turned out to be from the Moldavian Communist Party? On balance I thought probably not. But what a brilliant wheeze: tempt us into spying upon ourselves and charge us a tenner for the privilege.

Five weeks later I received a reply, reproduced below.

Dear Mr. Clark,

We have conducted a search of Security Service Records, and have determined that the Service does not process any personal data to which you are entitled to have access under section 7 of the [Data Protections Act]. You should not take this response to imply that the Security Service does or does not hold any personal data about you. This reflects the policy of successive Governments of applying the principle of "neither confirm nor deny" with regard to the activities of the security and intelligence agencies in the interests of protecting national security.

Yours sincerely,
Laurence Brett
Data Controller

For some reason I don't like the chummy way he uses his personal name, so I am going to call him "L." It was pretty clear what "L" was telling me: bugger off—I've trousered your tenner but I'm not going to tell you anything at all. Gee, thanks.

My options appeared to boil down to one of two things: either, like Norman Baker, I take MI5 to the High Court and force it to reveal whether or not it has a file on me—or I hang around the bars of Vauxhall in the hope of chatting up one of its officers and persuading her to have a quick peek through MI5's filing cabinets to see whether the dastardly organization has a file on me.

Let's get one thing clear: it is a happy country where one can speculate as to whether MI5 has a file on us, without any genuine fear that we will receive a midnight knock, followed by a stint in the salt mines. But I would still rather like to know whether there is a file on me in some deep dungeon below Westminster, if only to see whether I could recognize myself from it. The evidence, so far as I can tell, suggests I might just have some trouble.

James Bond has done the British security services, MI5 and MI6, a huge amount of good over the years. It has made everyone think that the archetypal British spy is a suave individual in successful pursuit of reclusive megalomaniacs. The reality is a little different. The government has appointed an "Interception of Communications Commissioner" to police the security services' use of phone-tapping and computer-hacking. Upon his retirement from the job in February 2007, Sir Swinton Thomas published his findings which painted a rather worrying portrait of a bunch of office-bound bunglers who would struggle to spy on a rice pudding, let alone penetrate Blofeld's lair. There were 3,972 occasions, he reported, when security services had sought a warrant to tap somebody's phone—and filled in the wrong number. So, instead of listening to Mohammed plotting a bomb atrocity from a bedsit in West London they had plugged into Ethel talking to her friend Mabel about her bunions.

Theoretically, the security services cannot bug our phones without the permission of the Home Secretary. But this only tells half the story. In a sense, all of our telephone conversations, faxes, and emails are monitored by the security services all the time. Over the last few years it has become increasingly clear that since the 1970s the security services of the USA, Britain, Australia, Canada, and New Zealand have been operating a vast listening machine called ECHELON, which is screening all telephone calls passing through those countries for signs of incriminating phrases or patterns of speech. In Britain, the main physical manifestation of this beast is the cluster of 30 white domes on Menwith Hill, North Yorkshire, but it relies on a network of sites throughout the member countries. You don't physically have to be in one of those countries for the system to monitor you: it could pick you up, for example, making a telephone call from Namibia to Chile if the call happens to be routed via Australia.

In 2000, the European Parliament was sufficiently interested in ECHELON (which raises the question: why the hell hasn't the EU got their own such program?) to commission a report into its activities. It was especially concerned about allegations that in 1994, the European consortium Airbus had lost out to Boeing on a $6 billion contract to supply planes to Saudi Arabia as a result of industrial espionage via the ECHELON system. The report didn't provide much in the way of enlightenment over that issue, though it did uncover some interesting tidbits. A former Canadian Secret Service employee told of the case of a woman who was picked up by ECHELON after she used an "ambiguous phrase" in a telephone conversation with a friend. As a result, her name, address and telephone number were added to a list of terrorist suspects. Presumably, the same could happen to any of us should we, by chance, happen to use a phrase which is known to be used as a code by a terrorist group.

Interestingly enough, the one body of people whom the security service is not keeping an eye on is Parliament. Under a law known as the Wilson Doctrine, introduced in 1966 by Prime Minister Harold Wilson, spies are forbidden from hacking into MPs' telephones. When Sir Swinton Thomas recommended that this rule be rescinded, pointing out that it put MPs above the law, the then-Prime Minister Tony Blair flatly refused. I am sure that the current crop of MPs is a thoroughly sound body of men and women to whom it would never occur to subvert the kingdom. But it just occurs to me: if one were an enterprising young terrorist, would it not be a good career move to get elected to Parliament—or maybe just to get a job as an MP's researcher, knowing that the telephones in the Houses of Parliament are safe from the pricked ears of the security services?

At least Britain's security services have yet to emulate the Canadian Police, which in 2004 had the cheek to suggest that telephone customers be subjected to a charge of 25 cents a month—to cover the cost of the police tapping their phones.

Maybe I would happily pay up if I could see my MI5 file. Like Big Brother, whom by the end of *1984* Winston Smith has come round to idolize, I sometimes wonder whether secretly we like the idea of being monitored and watched. I ask this because of the astonishing case of the East Germans who cannot quite seem to cast off the spell of their once-hated police force, the Stasi. After the fall of the Berlin Wall in 1989, many of the Stasi's 90,000 agents quickly realized that the game was up, and that among the many millions of documents stashed away was information that could end up incriminating them. The then-Stasi boss instructed his staff to embark on one of the biggest shredding operations in history, obliterating 45 million documents. Among them were logs and observations of six million East Germans—one in three of the population—who had been suspected of some kind of subversive activity.

One might imagine that East Germans would be grateful for this huge destruction of personal data, relieved that it could no longer be used against them. But that would be horribly to underestimate human curiosity. Within two years of the great shredathon, historians—encouraged by groups representing the victims of the Stasi—had begun the rather tedious business of piecing together some of the shredded documents. By 2007, Germany's federal commission for state security files had decided that it was going to piece together the whole damn lot—to which end it had employed one of the most intriguing inventions of our age: the "de-shredder." The machine sorts out fragments of paper according to the color and texture of the paper, and then pieces individual documents together—all at a fantastic speed. By 2013, East Germans will be able to satisfy their curiosity: was the Stasi really following them, or were they imagining it? What information was kept on them, and how accurate was it?

There is something rather delightfully Germanic about the whole exercise. Despite myself, I can understand the attitude of those who feared and loathed the Stasi and yet now are keen to see the documents which its officers compiled. I think had I been living in East Germany prior to 1989, I, too, would want to know whether the Stasi had followed me down Karl Marx Allee to the third coffee shop on the left, and what they had gathered of my conversation there. And worse, I think I would find it difficult to stop myself perversely wanting to know this even if I knew that the information was likely to reveal embarrassing details.

Who knows, maybe one day, even if "L" has tossed everything through the shredder, I will eventually get to see what information he was hoarding on me.

CHAPTER EIGHT

ME AND MY ID

"Like the railways in the 19th century or the National Grid last century, the national identity system will soon become part of the fabric of British life."

—**Home Office minister Liam Byrne** coming over all lyrical about the National Identity Cards Act 2006.

There is, of course, one small difference between railways, the public electricity supply, and ID cards. The first two innovations were jolly useful. Indeed, they transformed everyday life. It is rather more difficult to see the public utility of a plastic card telling us who we are and where we live. Most of us know that already. To have it on a little ID card may possibly make life a little easier for the police and one or two other public agencies, but it isn't going to take us on a day trip to Shrewsbury or make us a piece of toast.

In 2008, Britons applying for passports will begin to be issued with ID cards. Some time after 2010 they are likely to become compulsory. They will contain 50 pieces of information about us, including our name, date of birth, main address, any other addresses we use, all previous addresses, a photo, biometric data including a facial scan, an iris scan, and a fingerprint, plus any external characteristics that are capable of being used to identify us. They will not merely be cards: they will, when stuffed into a machine capable of reading them, link up to our entry on the national ID register. Every time any of the data changes—which includes us moving or buying a holiday home—we will be obliged to apply to the national ID register to have our cards updated. Failure to do so could land us with a £1,000 fine.

Collecting and storing this data will not come cheap. By 2007 the cost of setting up the ID card scheme had risen to a projected £5.75 billion. The cost to individuals, meanwhile, has risen to around £100 for an ID card-cum-passport (to put this into perspective, in 1995 a new passport cost £18). British citizens, as if one needed reminding, have not taken too kindly in the past to the concept of taxes on their mere existence. At the rate ID cards are going, soon they will be as much a burden to the poor as was the ill-fated poll tax when introduced in 1990—dropped, the government should take note, after riots. At least the poll tax helped pay for schools and trash collection. Your £100 ID card bill will pay for... er, a piece of plastic.

Moreover, ID cards promise to cause considerable disruption to our lives. In order to supply the information it will be necessary for us to attend an interview at which we will be measured and photographed. In 2005, the government undertook trials involving 2,000 volunteers, hand-picked to represent the general population, who were individually surveyed for the biometric information which will be registered on the cards. Each was given a facial scan, an iris scan, and had their fingerprints recorded. The result? It took an average of seven minutes and 56 seconds to record the information. To extend this process to all 60 million Britons will take 905 man-years.

And that is only the beginning. After being measured for their biometric data and issued with ID cards, the volunteers were then subjected to the process of proving that they were the holder of the card. Each was scanned again and the information compared with the information recorded on the card—rehearsing the process that in years to come will be routine as we pass through airport security, passport control, claim welfare benefits, and any number of other familiar tasks. How long did it take for ID cardholders to prove that they were the person whose information was recorded on the card? Anything from 39 seconds to 80 seconds. It might not sound a lot, but put it into the context of a crowded airport arrivals lounge or a cross-channel ferry port, and it will cause huge delays.

And that is when things are working well and the machines can identify us. For much of the time they will not—as the 2005 trials proved. To prove a positive match between the iris scan of the cardholder and the iris scan recorded on the card worked in 96 percent of cases. To do the same with fingerprints worked in 80 percent of cases. Comparing facial scans worked in only 69 percent of cases. Worse, the success rates plummeted with disabled people: iris scans worked in 91 percent of cases, fingerprints in 80 percent of cases, and facial scans in just 48 percent of cases. In other words, the disabled stand to become disadvantaged still further as they struggle to identify themselves. It is hard to imagine that this is what the government intended when it first proposed ID cards.

In response to these lousy results, the government argued that the technology was still under development. I am sure it is. But one might have hoped that, with just three years to go before the first card was due to be issued, the process of issuing and checking ID cards might just be a little slicker than this. You can guess what it will mean: roomfuls of unfortunate individuals at airports, benefit offices, and the like, whose identity cannot be proved by the ID card reading machines and who are left waiting in bureaucratic limbo as a result. Just where do you start when you can't actually prove that you exist?

By the way, if you think the obvious deduction from the above results is that iris scans should be used as the sole biometric data on ID cards—and fingerprints and facial scans dropped—it is not quite as straightforward as that. One of the problems is that relying on iris scans to prove identity will discriminate against particular groups of people. Iris scans proved especially difficult to record in the case of black people and the over-60s. As for fingerprints, these proved difficult to record and check in the case of people with fat fingers. It is perhaps a blessing that the famously well-fed King of Tonga died last year at the age of 88. Relations with the Southern Pacific kingdom could have been soured forever, had he been forced to enter the dystopian netherworld of Heathrow passport control.

But even if the cards were to identify us correctly, what would they achieve? One remarkable thing about ID cards is that the government has never seemed to know what exactly they are for. To start with, they were about the prevention of terrorism—the justification which the government highlighted after the London tube bombings of July 7, 2005. But the terrorists behind that outrage, like those behind 9/11, did not seek to conceal their identities, only their intentions. Indeed, terrorist organizations do not work by recruiting shifty individuals with false beards and fake names: they function by establishing cells of "sleepers" who merge into society and behave so as to arouse no suspicion until the moment they are called to do their deed.

Next, ID cards were about illegal immigration. This is a problem, but it has never satisfactorily been explained what ID cards would do to tackle it. How, for example, would the existence of ID cards help find the 11,077 foreign students revealed by *The Times* to have gone missing from their universities after being granted short visas to enter Britain? At present, noted the newspaper, the efforts made to find these missing students is virtually zero; most universities don't even bother to report missing students to the Home Office.

Then ID cards were supposed to be about social security fraud—until it was pointed out by the Conservative home affairs spokesman David Davis that 95 percent of benefit fraudsters do not lie about their identity, only about their circumstances.

One thing is for sure: as former MI5 chief Dame Stella Rimington has pointed out, ID cards are only any use if they can be proven to be impossible to forge. Given that, by the Home Office's own admission, 10,000 false passports—which themselves are supposed to be all but impossible to forge—were issued in 2006, this seems a forlorn hope. All these passports, like the coming ID cards, contained biometric data, and yet still fraudsters manage to reproduce them. As a clue to what is going on, the *Daily Mail*, employing the services of a skilled IT consultant, proved that it is possible to hack into the data contained within the passport by scanning the envelope in which the passports are delivered to their holders. Thus armed with the information, the holder's identity can then be stolen. Okay, it is a harder business than making a false version of a traditional passport, without biometric data. But the fact is that it can still be done. Passport holders are being put to massive trouble and expense, and given a false sense of security, when in reality they are still at risk from identity fraud.

The people who will lose out from the introduction of ID cards will not be criminals attempting to conceal their identities—who will have access to the finest forgery techniques available, and who will always be waved through checkpoints as a result, but ordinary people who find themselves without an ID card, either because they have lost it, had it stolen, or because it has failed to arrive in the post. The result will be bureaucratic limbo as they are unable to prove that they in fact exist—not to mention the £1,000 civil fines which the government has suggested will be imposed upon those who refuse or fail to obtain an ID card—or who merely fail to register changes in data on their cards, such as a change of address. Far from solving crimes, the ID card system will merely be a mechanism for creating them.

How are the police proposing to monitor 60 million ID card holders when they cannot even keep tabs on a few thousand prisoners who have been released into the community wearing electronic tags? According to Home Office figures obtained by the Conservative Party in 2007, one in nine tagged prisoners breaks his curfew. Between them, tagged prisoners are committing 2,500 crimes a year. In spite of this record I wouldn't put it past the government one day to decide that so many ID cards are being forged there is only one solution: to implant us all with an identity microchip—as many dogs already have been.

The irony is that once Britain was, among developed countries, the one most inclined to err on the side of privacy of the individual. While other European countries maintained an ID card after 1945, which in many cases had to be carried by the bearer at all times, Britain abolished its wartime ID card scheme in 1952. This occurred after Acting Lord Chief Justice Lord Goddard ruled that it was quite wrong for police to carry on demanding, for trivial purposes such as a motorist parking too long outside the butchers, a card that had been introduced for wartime security. "To use acts of Parliament," he ruled, "passed for particular purposes during war, in times when the war is past... tends to turn law-abiding subjects into lawbreakers, which is a most undesirable state of affairs."

It is a shame, before 60 million Britons are put through an expensive bureaucratic process that will achieve very little, that such wise counsel does not prevail today.

CHAPTER NINE

ME AND MY POCKETS

*"We are trying to fight 21st century crime—
anti-social behavior, drug-dealing, binge-drinking,
organized crime—with 19th century methods,
as if we still lived in the time of Dickens."*

> — **Tony Blair** in his speech to the Labour Party conference in 2005,
> shortly before proposing his latest initiative: stop and search powers
> that would effectively revive the search-on-suspicion ("sus") laws from
> the Vagrancy Act, 1824.

Among the many receipts for dry-cleaning and shoe repairs in my wallet,
I have a little ticket from the Sussex Constabulary. It is a small memento
from the day in 2004 when I was stopped and searched at Gatwick Airport
by a policewoman carrying a very large and frightening machine gun. One
doesn't argue with such weapons. Yes, of course, she could have a peek inside my bags (which, incidentally, had been through an X-ray machine not
half an hour beforehand). Satisfied I was carrying nothing of interest she
then offered me a little certificate saying where and when I was searched—
and the reason why. I am still fascinated by the reason she gave for searching me: she ticked a little box marked "Going near equipment." What kind
of exciting equipment do they have at Sock Shop, where I had been idly
browsing? Had I nearly stumbled by accident upon a surveillance camera

disguised as a pair of argyle socks? It was tempting to go back and have a fumble through the socks to see what I could find, but on balance I decided this might be unwise.

I was at first reassured when the officer wrote out a piece of paper saying where, when, and why I had been searched. Then it clicked: this was not for my benefit; she was creating a record of where I, this sinister Sock Shop browser, had been at a particular time. Had I been searched in Southend, that would have been recorded too. This is the element of modern "stop and search" that was absent from the old "sus" laws.

My experience at Gatwick was the second time I had been searched, as it happens. Keep skulking suspiciously around airport retail outlets and I shall soon have enough "stop and search" tickets to make a small quilt. The first occasion, in many ways, was more bizarre than the second. I was walking through a park in Derby, and emerged from a gateway to find myself confronted by two policemen who insisted on searching my pockets. Was there anything in particular they were looking for, I asked them? Yes: a number of plants had recently been stolen from the park. Fair enough, but just how do you sneak a rhododendron bush into your trouser pockets?

No one can say that "stop and search" is anything sinister and new. It is nothing if not good ol' fashioned policing; indeed, it is in many ways reassuring that it still goes on in an age when so much policing has been contracted out to cameras. Formal powers for the police to dip their hands into the pockets of passing members of the public date from the 1824 Vagrancy Act–the hated "sus" law. But it is something to which Britons are increasingly having to get accustomed. In the year 2004–05, 32,062 people were stopped and searched on Britain's streets, a nine percent increase in a year. Stop and search powers are contained within several acts of parliament, from the Crossbows Act to the Wildlife and Countryside Act.

For the most part, the police at least have to give a reason to search us–even if it is an improbable one like searching for rhododendrons in your pockets. However, if they are struggling to find a reason, they don't have to scratch their heads too long: they need only get a police dog to sniff over us. Since the London Underground terrorist attacks of July 7, 2005, police dogs have become a regular sight at tube stations, airports, and other public places, their apparent purpose being to sniff out explosives. Few would argue with the aims of the exercise, but there is scant sign that the pooches are much good at their task. In fact, you might as well employ a bat as a lookout. In a test on the Chicago railway system, a sniffer dog managed to miss a bag full of explosives placed six feet in front of its nose. There is no record of any dogs on the Underground having sniffed out explosives over the past couple of years. But they have proved pretty zealous at sniffing out illegal drugs. So much so, in fact, that they have a habit of barking at passengers who although not drug-users themselves, police conclude, have traces of drugs on their bodies because they have brushed past somebody who is.

In a study in New South Wales, 4,078 suspects were stopped and searched after a police dog trained to detect drugs showed a special interest in them. On closer inspection just 27 percent of those suspects were found to be carrying any drugs. Who knows why the dogs picked out the other 73 percent? Maybe they had detected faint traces of drugs on their clothes—a US study reveals that 80 percent of banknotes are contaminated with enough illegal drugs to excite a police dog. Or maybe the dogs themselves had snorted so much of their quarry that they were themselves suffering from drug-induced paranoia. But what, one has to ask, is the point of an animal that delivers such a high rate of false alarms?

There is a very good point, as it turns out. The law has established that when you are sniffed by a police dog it does not count as an official "stop and search" operation. But a bark from a sniffer dog does then constitute a reason for stopping and searching individuals by hand. And who knows what one might find then? In other words, the dogs' wayward noses are being used to justify more or less random police searches on the general public—"fishing expeditions," as they tend to be called.

Not that in many parts of Britain is it any longer strictly necessary for police to give a good reason for stopping and searching individuals. The Terrorism Act of 2000 enabled the government to nominate, for 28 days at a time, certain places where the police would be free to search anyone who took their fancy, at any time, giving no reason whatsoever. After the US terrorist attacks of September 11, 2001, the entirety of London was designated such a zone. No matter that the designation lasts only 28 days; every four weeks ministers simply sign a piece of paper that extends the powers for another four weeks.

Yet the extraordinary thing about surveillance powers is that once you start creating them they never seem to be enough. In May 2007, a leaked letter revealed that the government is planning, as part of a new counter-terrorism bill, to go one step further—and allow the police, everywhere and all the time, to search whoever they like, without reason. Moreover, those stopped would be obliged, under pain of a £5,000 fine, to give their identity and answer questions as to where they are going. Remarkably, this was not an initiative that seems to have started with the police; indeed, many officers expressed their concern that the government was contemplating such a law, when they felt they already possessed ample powers.

One would hate to "disarm" the police in the fight against crime, but shouldn't we listen to them before granting them powers they feel they don't need and which they think will end up souring relations between them and their employers, the general public? What, after all, is wrong with the police having to give a reason for stopping and searching an individual? At the very least it is basic courtesy. If they are looking for people carrying illegal knives, surely they can tell you that. If you fit the profile of a wanted terrorist, they can tell you that, too. To offer this kind of information does nothing to undermine their duty; but it does do something to allay suspicion.

Perhaps the real reason the government doesn't want us to know why we are being searched is that the reason is often so trivial. Towards the end of my brief conversation with the policewoman at Gatwick I had a good idea why she was really stopping me. What, she wanted to know, did I consider my ethnic group to be? She proffered me a list: White British, British Asian, Black and White African, Yellow and Pink-Spotted Polynesian Eskimo, and so on. I declined to say, even when her eyes opened wide with disappointment. Sorry, I said, but she would have to put me down as REFU—that is the category for refuseniks who, as is our right, decline to co-operate with this bureaucratic nonsense (I urge every citizen to describe themselves as a REFU in order to subvert the whole exercise). And off she went in search of someone else of the right skin color, to make up her ethnic quotas for the day.

One wonders how many of the 32,062 people stopped and searched by the police last year were searched for this same reason: to make up the numbers. We are less a surveillance society than a checkbox society, our pockets gone through at whim to meet some perverse target.

CHAPTER TEN

ME AND MY TRAVELS

"No passengers are obliged to submit to a search of persons or goods if they choose not to board our aircraft."

— Helpful announcement at a Canadian airport describing the Hobson's choice available to passengers.

In the spring of 2001, some friends of mine visited the United States for the first time. Upon arrival in the US they were met by a cheery customs official who checked their documentation, asked them to present first their mobile telephone and then their shoes to be treated with disinfectant. They puzzled for a while, then it clicked: at the time Britain was in the midst of a foot and mouth epidemic, which was to lead to the slaughter of several million farm animals. Foot and mouth, reasoned US customs—gee, we better disinfect all their phones and shoes. Needless to say, one could quite easily have stuffed one's mud-spattered boots in one's suitcase and no one would have been any the wiser.

Ah, those were the innocent days, a few months before the terrorist attacks of 9/11. Americans were able to board airliners much as they would the number 24 bus, with the minimum of fuss. Since 9/11, not entirely unreasonably, airports in the US and Europe have discovered security in a big way. Travelers are now requested to set aside two hours at airports in order to have themselves examined, inspected, their papers checked, and their bodies given a quick once-over. Passengers on many flights are now forbidden from taking on board so much as a bottle of ear ointment, for fear that it contains the ingredients of a DIY bomb. By August 2007, it was taking passengers an average of 90 minutes just to get through security, and that doesn't include the time it takes them to reach their boarding gate, or stand in another queue there.

Many passengers will be unaware of some innovations introduced since 9/11, such as the "millimeter wave scanners" now subjecting each passenger to a personal X-ray. "Nineteen out of 20 persons preferred a scan to an invasive pat-down physical search," reassures the website of the manufacturer of one such machine, ignoring the fact that invasive searches used to be inflicted only on a few particularly shifty-looking individuals or those whose body-piercings had set off an alarm, while every passenger is subjected to a millimeter wave scan. Perhaps the researchers might have got a different result had they shown exactly how they appear to a security officer surveying a millimeter wave scanner screen: naked.

One doesn't quibble with all this extra security lightly, though some of it appears to be driven as much by the needs of commerce as security: what is the point of confiscating every last pair of tweezers and nail scissors from the hand luggage of passengers if shops the other side of the security barriers are selling the same items? It took a failed attack on Glasgow airport in June 2007 (involving a car packed with explosives driven into the terminal building) for authorities to realize that by creating lengthy security queues in airport buildings they are creating a target for terrorist attack. Why bother struggling to get on a plane when here, in the departures hall, are several hundred potential victims all nicely packed together?

Airline security, needless to say, does not begin and end with searches inside airport buildings—and neither should it. The security checks begin the moment you purchase your ticket. Click the "purchase ticket" button on an airline's website and your details will immediately be forwarded to the Pentagon for inspection, so that you can be assessed for the risk you present to the flight. It is all very well—except that the computers have not proved to be so very brilliant at their job.

Imagine the embarrassment, not to mention the fear. You board an airliner heading to the United States. Three hours into the flight, over the mid-Atlantic, the pilot suddenly announces over the intercom that the flight is being aborted and that the plane will be turned around and head back to Heathrow "for security reasons." The passengers are mutinous. The only blessing is that they don't—and you don't, for the moment—realize that it is you who are the cause of the security alert. The reason? Your name matches that of a terrorist suspect. You've never had a murderous thought in your life, let alone had your elbows in a bowl of Semtex, but thanks to the unfortunate accident that your birth name matches that of a suspicious character, you and your fellow passengers are forced into making a 2,500 mile detour back to Heathrow, and the frustrations of beginning your journey again.

Impossible? Unfortunately not. It happened to a passenger on a British Airways flight to New York in January 2005. And it could, of course, happen again—anytime that a computer in the US Department of Homeland Security puts two and two together and gets five.

The offending system in the above case was the database of Passenger Name Records, which contains information collected from passengers when they book their flights. If I book a flight to the US tomorrow I will have to give my name and address, and divulge my credit card number to pay for the flight. I may also have booked onward flights, hired a car or booked train or coach tickets, giving a clue as to my itinerary while I am in the US. I may have booked with frequent flyer miles, giving details of all my previous flights. I may also have booked a special meal, be it vegetarian, kosher or halal. All this information—indeed 34 pieces of data—will be used to check my details against those of people on wanted lists, and give me a score relating to the risk it believes I pose to the flight. Too bad if my plane is already in mid-Atlantic: there is no way that I am going to be allowed to land in the US if my details—even by accident—are any kind of match for those of a terror suspect.

But your name doesn't have to match that of a terrorist to place you under suspicion. Passenger Name Record data, the US Department of Homeland Security acknowledged in June 2006, is being fed into its Automated Targeting System, which cross-checks with other databases and gives each passenger a numeric score that is supposed to correspond to the risk that the passenger poses to the US. It isn't pinpointing known terrorists, in other words, but profiling all passengers to see whether they match Washington's preconceived image of a terrorist. Inevitably, however, such a system discriminates against those who, without planning to blow up a single US citizen, simply want to travel in a slightly unusual fashion. Thanks to the Automated Targeting System it is now effectively illegal for a tourist to travel to the US without booking a package tour, or having something else to prove that their trip has been planned in detail.

Strangely, the US does not apply this risk-profiling to people buying guns. Indeed, like Cho Seung-hui, who gunned down 32 staff and students at Virginia Tech in April 2007, you can be a megalomaniacal nutcase with murderous fantasies and still go out and buy a 9-mm Glock pistol. Yet turn up at US immigration control without a travel itinerary and you are liable to be led off in chains as a suspected terrorist. Talk about a lack of proportion.

The European Union has been fighting the US authorities for three years over the handling of Passenger Name Records. There is a case, the EU believes, for handing a certain amount of information over to the US. But my meal preferences? Why does the US Department of Homeland Security need to know whether I don't eat chicken or I am allergic to peanuts? Fatuous maybe, but the information might also at some point be misused: what, for example, does it tell you about a passenger who ordered a halal dinner?

It isn't just foreigners flying into US airports who are being screened in this way. The US government runs a Computer-Assisted Passenger Pre-Screening System to monitor the movements of US citizens traveling around the country by air—and which it plans to extend to trains, buses, and ferries. The UK, too, has embarked on its own system, Project Semaphore, a £15 million pilot scheme to monitor those who enter and leave the country—or as the Home Office self-importantly puts it—a "comprehensive passenger movement audit trail."

One of the problems of collecting and storing so much data is that it has a horrible tendency to go missing. An American pressure group, the Privacy Rights Clearinghouse, keeps a log of the astonishing number of occasions when data collected by US government departments and private companies has gone missing. In one case Georgia's state government sold off surplus computers without cleaning the hard disks, allowing the purchasers access to credit card numbers and social security numbers, a gift to fraudsters. The Department of Agriculture, in a reply to a request under the Freedom of Information Act, managed to reveal personal financial details of 350,000 individuals. The theft of a laptop from the US Department of Veteran Affairs allowed thieves potentially to view social security numbers and other data on 28 million military veterans. And so it goes on. What use are systems designed to improve security if they are so leaky that they actually make individuals more vulnerable to fraud?

Snooping into the plans of travelers is not novel. Some early rail tickets in the 1830s and 1840s required passengers to record the purpose of their visit—so, obviously, if you wrote "to rape the occupants of the Ladies' waiting room at Bath Spa" you could easily be identified by the authorities. But the mania for collecting data on our travel plans has reached such a height that it has become difficult to travel if one's journey does not fit what authorities consider to be a normal pattern.

When I travel, I like to do so in a spontaneous fashion. I want to move around at whim, visit wherever takes my fancy, and if I feel like it at a later date, write about what I've seen and sell the piece to a newspaper. Within Europe this presents no problem whatsoever: I get waved off the ferry by an apathetic customs official, after which the entire Shengen area (a collection of countries which have decided to pool their policing of immigration) is at my disposal without so much as a customs formality. If I attempt to travel in this fashion in the US, on the other hand, I will not only run into petty bureaucracy: it will be virtually impossible for me to make such a trip legally. First, US customs does not like wandering foreign visitors. If I wish to visit America, the US Embassy tells me, I am "strongly advised" to provide details of pre-booked accommodation. If I do not, and US officials are unable to glean details of where I plan to stay from my Passenger Name Records, I am warned menacingly that I will be "required to pursue this matter with US Immigration."

What is it all supposed to achieve? Singling out travelers without a detailed itinerary wouldn't have stopped the 9/11 hijackers, who entered the US to enroll on pre-booked flying courses. If I were a terrorist trying to gain entry to the US to explode a bomb I would quickly work my way around the system by booking myself on a package tour—a kind of latterday Baedeker raid. In fact, perhaps there is a market for such tours:

'Milwaukee and the Great Lakes'

Day 1
You will settle into your sumptuous hotel in the city center. After a coach tour of the central districts, you will have a free afternoon to explore downtown, followed by a five course dinner.

Day 2
You will join a coach trip to explore the western shores of Lake Michigan, with optional Port Washington add-on.

Day 3
After a morning excursion to tour the Bridges of Madison County, you will enjoy a free afternoon's shopping. After a farewell to your fellow guests and the hotel, you will be driven to the airport where there will be plenty of time to explode your suitcase bomb in the departure lounge.

Secondly, there is the matter of my profession, journalism. British tourists may—for the moment at least—enter the US under the visa waiver scheme. But if I have a vague idea that I might at some point in the future use my experiences to write a piece for a newspaper, the US Embassy warns that I must apply for a visa—or rather one of about five different classes of visa. I think I get the picture, though the rules read just a little bit like John Cleese's schoolmasterly instructions to his pupils to "move your clothes down onto the lower peg immediately after lunch, before you write your letter home, if you're not getting your hair cut, unless you've got a younger brother who is going out this weekend as the guest of another boy..." If I am going to the US to write a news report, I am advised I may apply for an "I" visa. But if the report "falls into the category of entertainment"," I am warned that I must instead apply for an "O," "P," or "H" visa. As to what constitutes entertainment, I am advised to discuss my intentions with US immigration officials.

Oh, and if I am intending to write a piece about my travels but do not have a contract with a newspaper (which I don't) I must go through the process of applying for a full "B-1" business visa. This costs $100 and requires a trip to the US Embassy in London at a prescribed time—and all just to write a little piece about San Francisco in the spring. What if I don't bother? What if I travel to the US under the visa waiver scheme, and the US tax authorities later pick up on a piece I have written using my experiences there? Technically, I will have been working illegally, and will face arrest on any subsequent trip to the US.

I don't know how seriously the US immigration service takes such breaches of the code, and I can't say I intend to find out, but I am pretty certain that this kind of petty bureaucracy will not help snare a single terrorist. As with so many other forms of surveillance, governments are drowning under such a weight of data that one wonders whether they are losing touch with the job at hand.

I wouldn't be surprised if terrorist suspects are disappearing into the sea of data collected from airline bookings—in much the same way, in fact, as our suitcases. Here is an extraordinary statistic: according to estimates from the Association of European Airlines in the three months from April through June 2007, the six largest European airlines between them lost 1.12 million passengers' bags. This, at a time of heightened security, when the movement of every passenger and every bag is supposedly monitored at every step. How come, in the midst of this security, over a million bags can go vamoose? And where the hell are they? Are they spattered over the entire European landmass having fallen out of the sky? Is there some vast pile of them in the sewers beneath Heathrow, or what?

All I know is that there is something rather peculiar about a surveillance society that collects mountains of data on what we choose to eat on the plane and tracks our every movement around Sock Shop but is unable to keep tabs on something as physical and as obvious as our labeled bags.

CHAPTER ELEVEN

ME AND MY COMPUTER

"All I have to say is Wow! I no longer need be concerned that my loved ones will stumble upon things I have viewed."

— Testimony from nervous customer of a software company that offers to clean hard disks—software the British government proposed to ban.

I should have known better than to give away my intentions for my day out in Southend by typing the words "Southend Pier" into Google before I set out on my journey. I wanted to know the layout of the town and pier so as to plot a route which avoided the most obviously public areas, but in doing so I blew my cover.

I had a good idea of what happens every time we search the internet.

One morning in 2005, I received an email which appeared to come from the FBI. "Your computer," it read, "has been linked with more than 30 illegal websites. Please answer our questions." These questions, it turned out, were on a form I was invited to download. I didn't know whether to be worried, or flattered. What had I done that was so interesting as to have caught the attention of spooks across the Atlantic? Was it something to do with the occasion I innocently googled "horse" and "bedding" and was treated to some lurid photos á la Catherine the Great? Had I pressed the wrong key and accidentally hacked into the Pentagon computer?

No such luck. Fortunately, before I opened the attachment I smelled a rat and thought it unlikely that the FBI would approach me in this way: wouldn't they contact Scotland Yard, who would send round a team of heavies to break down my door at 5 a.m.? A little research revealed that the email very likely concealed a virus, disguised in a form calculated to catch the attention of those who spend hours guiltily trawling the nether regions of the internet. The creation of the virus, it turned out, had been greatly aided by the bizarre decision of the FBI to sell off domain names ending with ".fbi.gov" to commercial interests—enabling anyone to pose as a spy.

What on earth were they doing? Turning the FBI into a marketable brand must rank as one of the dumbest acts ever. It is just what you want, isn't it: the likes of President Kim Jong Il to snap up a .fbi.gov domain name so he can tease information out of unsuspecting US government employees.

The incident did get me thinking, though: can organizations really spy on my computer in the way that this email suggested the FBI was doing? Yes, they can. And what's more, they do. We know as much because in August 2006, the internet provider AOL released—by mistake, it insists—a mass of data relating to 20 million internet searches performed by 657,000 of its members over the preceding month. The data, it explained, was kept for "research" purposes, but was never intended to be released to the general public.

The general public certainly had an entertaining time snooping on AOL users' habits. One user had punctuated his online searches for finance sites and medical sites offering information on high blood pressure with searches for escort agencies in various cities worldwide. Others, possibly imagining that surfing the web on a personal computer in the privacy of their own home was a more private environment than thumbing through the magazines on the top shelf of their local newsagents, betrayed lurid sexual interests. One user seemed to have developed a desire to "commit suicide by natural gas." One can only imagine the rich pickings for police forces—and also for commercial organizations wanting to establish spending patterns.

The information was, theoretically, anonymous, the name of each user having been replaced with a seven digit number. But that didn't prove much of an obstacle to an enterprising reporter from the *New York Times* who decided to delve a little deeper into the search habits of user number 4417749, whose internet searches showed a certain interest in "numb fingers," "termites," and "dog that urinates on everything." More revealingly, in a way, the user had searched for "landscapers in Lilburn, Georgia" and had made several other local searches, which enabled the reporter to identify the user as Thelma Arnold, and the incontinent dog as Dudley.

Well, thanks to the *New York Times* for revealing the potential for misuse of personal data by internet providers and anyone else who has access to their data. Or thank you—up to a point. I just wonder what the newspaper could do with the personal data it wrung out of me while I was registering with its website in order to read more about the above story. What, it wanted to know, apropos nothing, "is your household income?" Who says the American press doesn't do irony?

Whenever I undertake a search on AOL, it transpires, the company keeps a record of it for a month. If I search on Google, the company will keep the data for two years—worldwide, that means that Google is storing details of around 100 billion searches. In some ways it is comforting to know that if I search Google for "tart" and "Amsterdam," it is unlikely to stand out among the other 100 million searches. But it is a little disconcerting nonetheless. Quite why Google keeps the data this long is the subject of an enquiry by Richard Thomas, Britain's Information Commissioner. He shouldn't have to look too far: one of the reasons internet providers keep details of our web searches is that the government demands they do, for at least 12 months. What's more, the government in 2005 lobbied the European Parliament, which demanded that data on internet searches be deleted after 12 months, to develop a Europe-wide standard for the period which internet companies must keep our records for.

But even if Google stopped storing details of my online searches, you can be sure that someone else will be storing them. Any website I visit may, unknown to me, be equipped with "web bugs" enabling the organizations that run them to obtain the IP address of my computer, allowing them to tell that I have been visiting the site. Even if I could disguise my IP address, I'm afraid I wouldn't be able to keep myself anonymous for long.

Many of those AOL customers whose data was inadvertently released to the public have exposed themselves by the chronically vain practice of regularly typing their own names into AOL's search engine, so that their log of searches reads something like:

Airline timetable, Minneapolis
Hotel, Kansas City
Jefferson R Seersucker III
Car hire, Miami
Flowers by mail
Jefferson R Seersucker III
Bondage
Jefferson R Seersucker III
Real Estate, Pennsylvania
Sex, horses
Jefferson R Seersucker III

And so on.

We are all at it, apparently—typing our names into Google, that is. In fact, I have long come to realize that I am part of a worldwide, virtual community of Ross Clarks. There is Ross Clark Material Handling and Ergonomic Solutions of Rancho Cordova, California, for a start—who went out and snapped the domain name rossclark.com before I got round to it. It seems to sell conveyor belts and forklift trucks. It could be worse, I suppose. In fact, it could be a lot worse. And by the way I'm sorry to the Australian poet, the Merseyside artist, the Scottish footballer, the New Zealand musicologist and the US sewerage engineer if you have lost business because potential customers, spying-by-Google, confused me with you.

It is fascinating to know that all these Ross Clarks exist, but also a little disconcerting, too. My chances of being mistaken for a namesake, or someone who shares the same birth date, or someone whose national insurance number is one digit different from mine and was wrongly entered on a form years ago, are high. Increasingly employers, credit agencies, private investigators, and many others are turning to the internet to find information out about us to vet us for various purposes. But what if the information is wrong? If we get turned down for a job, as some have been, on the grounds that a vetting turned up a criminal record we never knew we had, how do you go about correcting information that someone has picked up on Google, when you don't know what it is, where to find it, and who put it there?

Snooping on our computer habits is not always a bad thing. Who would cavil at the practice of security services searching the hard disks of terror suspects in the hope of foiling future atrocities? Who would not support attempts to identify and prosecute users of child pornography? In 2002, the US National Crime Squad rumbled an internet portal called Landslide, which for £21 a month gave users access to 300 websites carrying images of underage sex. Some 6,500 Britons were identified as having paid to see the images, most of whom were subsequently arrested in what the police termed Operation Ore. If it helped to stop sexual abuse of children that has to be a good thing—though the 32 suicides which have resulted from the inquiries are the downside of the hysteria which they have unleashed.

The use of computer data to nail terrorists and child porn-users is not without difficulties, however. It might not have been you who put the incriminating evidence on your computer, but someone else who had access to it for a few minutes. You might not even be aware that there is illegal material on your hard disk: how can you be sure that no one has touched your workplace computer while you went out for lunch?

You don't have to use the internet very long before you realize that it is a frightening place where the user can lose control of what appears on your screen—and, as a result, is imprinted on his hard-drive until the device is physically destroyed. What hope for any of us if the avalanche of email spam inviting us to have a peep at some unclad young lady can be collected and used against us?

Astonishingly, there seems to be little to protect innocent people from the prospect of disgrace. In February 2007, Julie Amero, a secondary school teacher in Norwich, Connecticut, was convicted for exposing her 12 year old pupils to pornographic images, an offense which carries a maximum jail term of 40 years. It wasn't just the length of the possible jail term—out of all proportion to the offense—which raised eyebrows. Julie flatly denied that she deliberately accessed any pornography on the class computer. The machine had, she maintained, been infected with malicious software which will be familiar to many computer-users: the porn had appeared as a succession of pop-up boxes which she had neither sought, nor could manage to close down. The computer, she believes, was infected when two of her pupils visited a seemingly innocent hairdressing site.

In her trial it emerged that the software which the police had used to investigate the offense could not distinguish between an unsolicited pop-up image and an intentional visit to a website. In other words, not just in this case but in every other case where computer-users have been convicted of downloading illegal images, there is no way in which prosecutors can distinguish between websites deliberately visited and those which the computer has been directed to visit by malicious software.

Julie Amero's conviction was later overturned in a higher court. But I suspect few computer-users—certainly not in Britain—have awoken to the danger that the misuse and misinterpretation of data on their hard disks could present. Occasionally when I visit the municipal recycling center I have a sly peek at the computers which have been dumped there. Yes, most still contain hard disks. Presumably, the owners have failed to appreciate the personal data which they have left behind. They might think that they have deleted private correspondence, passwords, and pin numbers, but unless they have literally destroyed the hard disk, the information remains on it somewhere and can easily be fished out by a geek with the right software.

What especially bothers me about the routine seizure of computer hard disks is the opportunities it presents for lazy policing. Whatever the crime, a standard response by the police now seems to be: let's seize the suspect's computer and have a look. Even if they can't nail us for the crime under investigation there is, of course, always the chance they might catch us out for something else. A recent terror raid resulted not in terror charges—which seemed far-fetched—but in computer porn charges. What is happening is that criminal inquiries are turning into fishing expeditions.

Maybe this exercise will occasionally result in the conviction of a terrorist or child-abuser. Rather more frequently, one suspects, it will result in prosecutions for minor offences which were detected as a result of frustrated investigators being unable to nail their suspects for the major crime which they were investigating. There is the potential, too, for searches of our Google habits to turn up fragments of innuendo that prosecutors can throw at juries in the hope of inviting them to put two and two together and make five. How do you feel that a Google search you might undertake to satisfy your idle curiosity into how bombs are made could one day be fished out of the thousands of other searches you have made online and used as evidence against you in a trial? It is all too easy to imagine oneself on a jury moved to convict a murder suspect because the terms "murder" and "life insurance" both appeared in his Google records—without stopping to wonder what others would make of our own Google records.

The awful possibility that information gathered about us from the internet could one day be used against us seems not to have dawned on computer-users generally. Far from being aware of the dangers, we make it remarkably easy for people to spy on us. From blogs to the voyeuristic MySpace. com, part of the Google empire, thousands of us seem quite happy to spew out personal information in the belief that no harm can come from it. Take the website MySpace. At first sight it appears a harmless piece of fun. Visit the site and tap in the words "the queen," and up will pop an entry filed by Her Majesty Queen Elizabeth II, who, in an unguarded moment, was persuaded that a modern monarch ought to converse with her subjects via the internet. Her Majesty, the entry informs us, "has 1,583 friends," among them a brown-nosing Tony Blair, who writes "this is the greatest honor to be included as one of your friends. You have been a great inspiration to me." You will also find a number of entries from people purporting to be Queen Elizabeth II, together with some entries from an altogether different sort of queen—such as "Tila Tequila," who is keen for us to view her upended in a thong. Less harmlessly—until MySpace removed them in July 2007—you also used to be able to find the personal profiles of, and make friends with, 29,000 sex offenders.

Her Majesty's entry aside, MySpace, and its rival Facebook, is essentially a forum for drunken college students who cannot conceive that any harm could ever come from disporting themselves in semi-naked poses for all the world to see. This is the generation for whom "Big Brother" is synonymous not with George Orwell's *1984* but with the British television program of that name, where a house-full of wannabe celebrities embarrass themselves for several weeks in the belief that all publicity is good publicity—indeed, the more excruciating their problems the more likely they are to land that latterday equivalent of the Victorian freak show—a mini TV series.

But do you want to bet that there is no such thing as bad publicity? Posting information and photographs about yourself on the internet can backfire spectacularly. In July 2007, Oxford University started sending emails to students whom it said it had caught engaging in "disorderly" end-of-term behavior—courtesy of images found on Facebook. One of the recipients, Alex Hill, received an email from proctors complaining that her Facebook entry carried a photograph of her covered in shaving foam in an Oxford street—an offense which under the university's regulations carries a potential fine of £75. "I don't know how the proctors got access to it," she complained. "I thought my privacy settings were such that only students could see my pictures." In the future, no one will be under such illusion: in September 2007, Facebook announced that it would be opening up personal details to all internet users, not just those registered with the site. It is rather as if one's private letters, diaries, and other cringe-making material were made available in all good book stores.

Oxford University is not the only organization to have developed an interest in trawling Facebook and MySpace. In 2007, a website called Viadeo surveyed the recruitment departments of 600 companies, asking them whether they had used the internet to do a little research on job applicants. It discovered that one in five did just this—tapping the names of would-be-employees into Google and looking them up on the likes of MySpace. Unsurprisingly, a few swiftly turned into won't-be employees. One firm reported that it had turned an applicant down after discovering her posing topless. Other applicants were rejected as a result of boasting about their drunken antics, or because they had developed a habit of complaining about previous employees on their blogs. One employee was rejected after a trawl of the internet revealed that he was on a police "wanted" list.

Why do we do it? Why do we make it so easy for the state, our employers and anyone else who is minded to, to spy on us via our computers? For me, I have come to the conclusion there is only one way to use a computer: assume at all times that there is a policeman peering over one shoulder and a criminal peering over the other. If one seems to be saying to you, "I wouldn't do that if I were you, Sir," or the other seems to say, "Thanks for the information, mate," it is time to slip out of cyberspace and do what Soviet dissidents learned to do: take to the streets to have their conversations, away, as far as possible, from the bugs.

By the way, even taking an ax to your computer won't necessarily mean the end of your data trail. Unknown to many computer-users—and quite possibly dismissed as an urban legend by some of those who have heard about it—most printer manufacturers have been persuaded by governments to program each machine with a unique code, invisible to the naked eye, which can be read in the event the police need to trace a suspect. Message to those in the habit of writing rude but anonymous letters to our leaders: under no circumstances return the warranty card to the manufacturers, because it will link you to every piece of paper that is ever printed from the machine—including anything printed by anyone who subsequently buys it from you.

CHAPTER TWELVE

ME AND MY CAR

"Stolen GPS devices lead cops straight to thieves' home."

— Headline about foolish US criminals who weren't
quite sure of the purpose of the Global Positioning System.

I have never been to the foyer of the headquarters of the Driver and Vehicle Licensing Authority (DVLA) in Swansea, Wales, but I wouldn't be at all surprised if it contained a large statue of Franz Kafka. From whom else can the organization have gained its inspiration? The life of Joseph K., though, was never as bizarre as that of Jane P. from Henley-on-Thames, who in 2004 was reported to have amassed 13 motoring fines for speeding, evading the London congestion charge, and parking on the pavement. Most of the offences, it turned out, had been committed in the London borough of Southwark—which Jane had never visited in her life.

She is not the only one. As Britain's traffic policing is steadily devolved to cameras and license-plate-reading software, there is an ever-growing body of motorists caught up in a nether world of mistaken identity. One Scottish milkman—whose electric milk truck had a maximum speed of 25 mph—was sent speeding fines relating to offences several hundred miles away from his round. A female motorist was stopped several times and obliged to try to prove that she had not stolen her own car; her registration number having somehow found its way onto a list of stolen vehicles.

Britain's surveillance society is frequently portrayed as a ruthlessly efficient machine, not least by the 1.8 million Britons who in 2007 added their names to a petition on the Prime Minister's website against the proposed use of road-pricing on British highways and beginning with the words: "The idea of tracking every vehicle at all times is sinister and wrong." But it seems to me that Big Brother could do with a new pair of specs. Clearly, a system of traffic policing based on license-plate recognition is only as good as the database which sustains it. And here lies the problem: the DVLA has admitted that records of 820,000 of the 33 million vehicles on its database are incorrect. Moreover, personal details of 7.8 million drivers are wrong, resulting in chaos and inconvenience for those wrongly accused of offences.

In some cases it is computer error that has caused this woeful inaccuracy. But there are other causes too. Eager to avoid speeding and parking fines, fraudsters have succeeded in "cloning" license plates of honest motorists. The fraudster commits the offences—and the honest motorist is sent the fines. One cannot, of course, eliminate the criminal tendency for good, but one might have expected the government to take into consideration the possibility of fraud before instigating a system of traffic policing that puts so much reliance on the reading of license plates.

The increasing use of speed and other traffic-enforcement cameras in Britain has led to accusations of a "police state"—mostly, it has to be said, among motorists who like driving fast and do not wish to be stopped from doing so. Describing British roads as a police state is rather wide of the mark. The use of cameras has coincided with a dramatic fall in the level of other traffic policing. Between 1999 and 2004, the number of drivers who were breath-tested by the police fell from 765,000 to 578,000—a period over which the number of deaths in alcohol-related accidents rose from 460 to 560. The chances of being breath-tested while driving in Britain are lower than virtually anywhere else in Europe. Nine percent of drivers have been tested in the past three years, in contrast to 64 percent in Finland and 33 percent in France. If we are living in a police state, it is one in which the police are remarkably invisible.

Or certainly less visible than the cameras that, as a sop to motorists who complain how jolly unfair it is that they have been caught, have been painted bright yellow. The result has, of course, been to render the cameras completely useless. I began this book by likening Britain's surveillance society to Jeremy Bentham's Panopticon, the prison designed to fool prisoners into thinking they were being watched constantly. But whoever it was who decided that speed cameras must be painted bright yellow seems to have misunderstood the panopticon principle. Stand by the side of a road near a speed camera and you see it happen over and over again: car after car braking furiously when the driver sees the camera, then accelerating away again once the white lines have been passed. I am not in principle against speed cameras, but I thought the idea was to catch people who drove too fast, not merely those who can't recognize the back end of a speed camera.

In spite of the obvious shortcomings of vehicle surveillance, the government's zeal is undimmed. It has recently committed itself to introducing a form of motoring taxation that will put us even more at the mercy of number plate recognition equipment and the DVLA's database. Instead of levying a tax on road fuel and making us buy a flat-rate vehicle license, the government wants to charge us for our use of the roads mile-per-mile—a system known as road-pricing.

This is fine in theory: you pay as and when you use the roads. The advantage of such a system is that the price can be adjusted according to the road and the time of day when you are traveling, thereby helping to smooth out traffic flows and cut congestion. The drawback is that such a system requires the use of complex technology to monitor the whereabouts of every vehicle at all times. The technology which would make this possible does exist, and indeed is already under test in several cities. It can be achieved either via a system of cameras capable of reading license plates or by global positioning technology, whereby every vehicle carries a tracking device.

Given the record of the London congestion charge, which at one point was consuming more in administrative costs than it was raising in revenue, how can the expense of setting up a country-wide network of number plate recognition cameras or satellite tracking devices really be justified when revenue could be raised much more cheaply through road tax?

The answer, as if we couldn't have guessed already, was given to us in July 2007, when the government announced that police would be given full, instant access to information from the cameras installed to support a road-pricing scheme. In other words, road-pricing has been a bit of a con all along. It has never been just about changing the way motorists are taxed; it has also been about monitoring our movements.

Even those who stick to the byways in an attempt to avoid being monitored will be caught sometimes: part of the plan is to install discreet cameras at every filling station in the country, the idea being that sooner or later every vehicle must fill up with fuel. It would be nice to think that one could still evade the cops by doing what a number of enterprising South Welsh motorists managed to do a few years ago: run their diesel cars on used cooking oil. (They didn't get away with it, by the way: reversing, for a while, the trend towards policing by cameras, the local constabulary sent officers onto the streets to sniff exhausts for the telltale aroma of burned chips.)

In a separate pilot scheme, the Department of Transport has approved a trial in which car registration plates will be fitted with Radio Frequency Identification Devices (RFIDs) as an alternative means of tracking the movements of every car in the country, without having to rely on temperamental license-plate-reading cameras. Or at least it will, presumably, until criminals, terrorists and any other wrongdoers who wish to evade capture work out where exactly on the number plate the RFID is and cut it off.

Regarding the 1.8 million-strong petition on the Downing Street website: just a word about the outcome. Did the government falter in its plans for road-pricing? Like hell it did. In return each for taking the trouble to register their objections, each signatory received a nice email from then-Prime Minister Tony Blair saying thank you very much—the government hasn't, you know, er, made a final decision on this, but look we've got to do something, etc. Whether it occurred to any of the signatories that there might be something a tad sinister about the government collecting a list of the names, addresses, and email addresses of opponents of its policies is another matter: I can think of a few countries where I wouldn't care to hand over such information—under pain of being enrolled on a course of re-education.

If you think this is far-fetched in a democracy such as modern Britain, you should consider what nearly happened in the case of protestors against Heathrow's third runway, which if built will obliterate a village to the north of the existing runway and lead to extra noise and annoyance in highly-populated surrounding districts. The runway, unsurprisingly, has drawn much opposition—not least because expanding the airport would appear to contradict somewhat the government's policy on global warming, which is to warn us grimly that we face meteorological Armageddon unless we cut greenhouse gas emission sharply in the next five years.

But whatever one thinks of the third runway, the reaction to the opposition by BAA, the company that owns Heathrow Airport, was something else. Faced with a seven-day protest by the "Camp for Climate Action" in August 2007, the company sought an injunction to prevent protesters approaching the airport, and from using public transport going to and from the airport. In doing so it named four individuals and several groups who have protested against expansion of the airport. One of them, Airportwatch, happens to be formed of a number of environmental charities including the National Trust and the Royal Society for the Protection of Birds, which between them have five million members. Although in court BAA did try to redefine its position—saying that it only wanted to exclude active protesters, the case does rather demonstrate the potential for using vehicle-tracking equipment. You signed that petition against the airport? You're not coming within five miles of the place, pal.

Even if the government does back down on its proposals for a road-pricing system based on number plate-reading or RFID technology, it won't be long before the necessary technology is available in another format. It is already becoming difficult to buy a new car that is not fitted with the Global Positioning System (GPS). This technology has been sold to the car-buying public on the promise that it will help them navigate, and help their car to be located should it be stolen. But don't forget that it can equally be used to track your location. The little gizmo sitting on your dashboard telling you to take the second left for Basingstoke is really a spy in your car. Don't be surprised if one day it is used to tax or trace you.

I didn't need to read the story about the owner of an £80,000 Mercedes who obeyed her GPS telling her to turn left, down a slipway and into the River Soar (nor the truck drivers who have got wedged on narrow bridges thanks to their GPS) to help me decide that I don't like this technology and I don't want it in my car. My scepticism is not widely shared, however. For most people, the benefits of electronic wizardry are so dazzling that they cannot see the downsides. Sometimes the benefits are an illusion: we would never believe a human who told us to drive into a river, but are quite happy to believe a machine that tells us to do this. Likewise police forces, security services, and other government agencies: they put faith in their surveillance equipment that they would never put in their staff.

This is a peculiar effect of surveillance, both on us and on our leaders: it gives the impression that everything is under control, when in fact it isn't. We think of a town center full of CCTV cameras as a place where no one can get away with crime, or an airport with barcoded baggage scanners as the ultimate in straight-through process efficiency—in spite of evidence that muggers still congregate in town centers and airports still lose suitcases with reckless abandon.

It is obvious where these controlling forms of technology are going to lead. The Japanese car manufacturer Nissan has experimented with a system which uses GPS to avoid collisions. A car fitted with the system can theoretically tell whether there are other vehicles headed on a collision course with it—say, emerging from a side street or from around a blind bend—enabling the driver to take avoiding action. It is also claimed that the system might allow drivers to avoid collisions with pedestrians—assuming, that is, that the pedestrian is carrying a mobile phone fitted with a GPS device.

One hates to point out snags, but do we really want to reach a situation where drivers feel they can waft along at any speed they fancy, comforting themselves that they will receive an automatic warning of any pedestrian around the next corner?

It certainly doesn't promise to make life safer for the poor sod who doesn't happen to carry a GPS phone wherever he goes.

CHAPTER THIRTEEN

ME AND MY HOME

"I just freaked out when you could see my pool."

— Visitor to Google Earth.

On the afternoon of Sunday June 22, 2003, I was mowing the lawn. My blue Peugeot 406 was parked on the driveway to my home, along with my grey Renault Megane and the cars of a couple of visitors to my house. You can look up this tranquil domestic scene if you want to—just visit Google Earth. It allows anyone with an internet connection to view images of the entire surface of the Earth.

I have to say I rather like Google Earth. It is certainly the quickest and safest way to go on holiday: transporting you across continents in seconds to have a peek at a sandy cove or to explore some tract of rainforest—without any fear of catching Delhi belly or even losing your bags. Sometimes I set the images moving at approximately 600 mph and at a height of 35,000 feet to simulate an intercontinental journey by jumbo jet. It brightens up a dull day.

Were I a wealthy homeowner fearful of burglary or kidnapping I am not so sure that I would appreciate the entire world being able to see the layout of my garden. On the other hand, I rather appreciate being able to home in on air bases in Iran; it does no harm—and quite possibly a lot of good—that ordinary citizens be allowed to join the Pentagon in its spying operations and see for themselves all those dodgy nuclear power plants.

I am rather less pleased that tax collectors should be using satellite photography to spy on my house. In a parliamentary answer in May 2007, Treasury Minister John Healey revealed that the Valuation Office Agency, which assesses British domestic properties for their taxable value, has a library of photographs of 823,000 British homes—properties whose size and value cannot easily be assessed from the public road. In Northern Ireland, for example, satellite images have already been used to assess the value of properties for council tax purposes—each property being subject to an annual levy of 0.63 percent of its value. The images, which are produced on a scale of 1:1250, are taken from an oblique angle in order to allow valuers to count the number of windows, as well as to assess the floor area of each property and have a peek at additions such as conservatories and swimming pools. The images can also be used to assess the value of the cars on the driveway, a factor which influences the value of homes in a neighborhood.

Satellite images of farms are of compelling interest to various government agencies, being used to identify farmers who fraudulently claim subsidies for crops which do not exist, and who burn materials which they should not be burning. Sometimes, the response has been less than polite. Home in on a field at Woodhouse Mill near Sheffield (53° 21' 50.57"N, 1° 20' 02.03"W) and you can see the worse "Arse" clearly carved into the corn. Maybe we should all take a lesson from this: how about we all plant up a flowerbed which, when viewed from the air, reads "Get lost, taxman"?

But for the government it is not enough simply to peer at the outside of our homes. It wants to know what is going on inside too. The government has proposed that in the forthcoming 2011 census, British homeowners will be asked to state whether there is any outstanding maintenance work required in their home—interesting information for future students of our DIY habits, no doubt, though one just wonders whether the information might also find its way into the paws of social workers, who will jump on an admission that the stair rods need replacing as evidence that our children are not safe in our home and would be better taken into care to help meet the government's adoption targets.

The government has already made a start towards the routine inspection of our homes. Any British homeowner putting a four-bedroom property on the market since August 1, 2007 has first had to compile a Home Information Pack. To do this you have to commission an "energy assessor" to come and measure up your home and issue it with an "Energy Performance Certificate"—a piece of paper giving the property a rating out of 100 for energy efficiency, plus a series of recommendations of how the home could be altered to consume less energy. The idea is that buyers will balk at the idea of buying a poorly-insulated home, thus forcing the seller to undertake some energy-saving alterations, thus helping to cut carbon emissions. Alternatively, given what we know already of how Prime Minister Gordon Brown operates, we can look forward to paying higher property taxes if our home is judged to fall beneath required insulation standards.

How useful the information will be is another matter. Curious to find out, I had two Energy Performance Certificates awarded to my home, each by different energy assessors. The result? One gave my home 32 out of 100 and the other 42 out of 100—that is the result of what is supposed to be a standardized assessment procedure, which the government has spent several years developing.

That is the problem with so much of the information gathered by surveillance. Not only is it intrusive; it is also of doubtful worth. In 2000, much to the chagrin of celebrities who moaned about loss of privacy and/or kidnapping, the Land Registry announced that it would make public the sale price of every property sold in England and Wales. No longer would we be left wondering what the Smiths paid for their semi-detached house down the road: we could look it up. There is a legitimate reason for this information to be made public: it prevents estate agents from talking us into paying too much for our homes. If we can see what number 23 Acacia Avenue sold for last July we are less likely to be fooled into paying too much for number 24. Moreover, there are a number of corrupt estate agents who have been caught fraudulently undervaluing the homes of elderly clients, so that the properties can be sold to an accomplice, then quickly sold on at a great profit. Putting information on sale prices in the public domain makes it more likely that such frauds will be exposed.

However, such information is only useful in preventing fraud if it is accurate and comprehensive. In practice, Land Registry data has proved to be neither. A large number of sales simply don't show up on the Land

Registry, either because the owners of the properties wrapped them up in limited companies—the purchase and sale of which does not have to be declared to the Land Registry—or because lawyers acting for the sale simply failed to pass on the information about sale price to the Land Registry. The Land Registry tells me "we are not required to police the system." What use is a system designed to fight fraud if fraudsters can easily keep the vital information from it, and the body charged with maintaining the database refuses to police it?

Interestingly, when in 2004 the Land Registry decided to sell the information on its database to commercial organizations—who could then exploit our nosiness by inviting us to look up the price which our friends, and various celebrities, paid for their homes, the price paid by then-Prime Minister Tony Blair for his home in Connaught Square, London somehow failed to make it on to these websites. "Although the registered titles still show the price paid it is possible that the information was deleted subsequently," a spokeswoman for the Land Registry tells me, but was unable to explain why or by whom the information had been deleted. Isn't it fascinating how a few gain a right to privacy and others do not? I hope I am not breaking state secrets to reveal that Mr. Blair paid £3.65 million for the property.

In a paper for the Center of Policy Studies in 2007, lawyer Harry Snook revealed that the state can now rely on 266 different pieces of legislation for powers to enter your home. That startling figure has to be put into context: many of the powers, it transpires, involve agricultural land rather than houses or apartments, and so are not strictly rights to enter your home. Moreover, on closer inspection, some of them do not involve intrusion. For example a right-of-way officer in the process of inspecting a public footpath is only exercising the same right to access as can be exercised by any member of the public.

Some of the powers quoted by Snook are long-standing: for example those contained within the Incitement to Disaffection Act (1934) and the Hypnotism Act (1952). But there is something rather disturbing about the way in which rights to enter our homes are almost routinely written into new legislation. When Council Tax replaced the short-lived Poll Tax in 1991, legions of surveyors were sent out onto the streets to value properties from the exterior (every property being put into one of eight bands and the tax applied progressively). Sixteen years on, the government argues that the time has come for a revaluation. Only this time it has decided that valuation officers must be given the right to enter our homes—just in case there turns out to be something inside the property, not visible from the road, that increases the value of the home. Why do they need to do that? It would be vastly cheaper if valuation officers were simply to revalue properties, using the Land Registry, every time a property was sold.

Perhaps valuation is not the only reason why the government wants to create these new powers. Will valuation officers really only be seeking to put a value on our homes; or, while they are there, might they also be looking out for building work that has been completed without planning permission or building regulations approval, for signs that the inhabitants might be living beyond what the taxman calculates to be their means, or for illicit lodgers? On past form, it is not difficult to work out where this is potentially leading: to the routine examination of our homes. There is a very big difference between a police officer entering a property because there is evidence of a serious crime being committed within and officials embarking on speculative "fishing expeditions" to see what they can hook.

The weird thing is that where there is clearly a case for a uniformed agent of the state to come into our home—such as to keep an eye on bailiffs who are seeking to seize our property to settle consumer debts—the government goes out of its way not to interfere. In 2007, the government tabled the Tribunals, Courts, and Enforcement Bill, under which bailiffs will be granted the power to break into domestic property and seize property in order to settle consumer debts without any need for a police officer to keep an eye on them and check that they stay within the law. Isn't this bizarre: the government seeks every excuse to nose around our homes, except when an army of privateers comes to collect debts run up by the unwitting clients of conmen and loan sharks. In this case the government tells us, sorry, but why should the police be bothered to come round just to check your house isn't ransacked and your knees broken?

CHAPTER FOURTEEN

ME AND MY MONEY

"Your privacy is important to us."

> — Statement on the website of a bank that sends out unsolicited
> mailings for credit cards, which can easily be filled in by people
> intercepting the addressee's post.

One of my most pleasurable early memories is of walking along a sidewalk aged 10 when suddenly in front of me, out of a side street, fluttered a £1 note. I am afraid I pocketed it. And no, I still don't feel guilty. That is both the advantage and disadvantage of real money: it is easy to find and easy to lose. Save for fingerprints and traces of cocaine (found on 80 percent of US banknotes), a £5 note or a dollar bill can pass through the economy without being traced—or, in many cases, being taxed. Only if one starts trying to deposit the swag from a great train robbery in a High Street bank—and a keen-eyed cashier notices that the serial numbers tally with the missing currency—is one likely to establish a data trail. As for coins, they are not numbered—as far as I am aware nobody has a clue as to where any particular twopence has been.

This, if some have their way, will soon change. In March 2007, Peter Ayliffe, chairman of Visa Europe, declared that by the year 2012 the European Union will be a cashless society. Instead of going round with a pocket full of grubby coins we will instead pay for everything, as we already do for large items, with cards. The only difference is that for items below £10 we will not have to enter a pin number or write a check; we will simply swipe our cards past a sensor, and it will automatically deduct the fee from our prepaid account.

The technology to run this kind of system already exists. If you travel by public transport in London you may use an "Oyster" card. This is a prepayment card: you place some credit on it; then, every time you travel, the card is debited with the cost of the journey. The card is now being extended beyond transport to participating shops. The coffee chain Starbucks has also experimented with its own prepay card—which was taken up by 100,000 customers in a couple of months.

It is simple to use, and promises to save us the bother of having to mend the holes in our pockets caused by heavy coinage. But there is a fundamental difference between cash and prepayment cards. The latter can be used to trace our every purchase, and with that our every movement. It is not hard to see why governments should be in favor. The elimination of cash would spell ruin for the black market. Who would risk evading their taxes knowing that with every transaction they were leaving a data trail which could lead to their conviction?

It is unlikely that Mr. Ayliffe will be proved right in his prediction—at least not in the timescale he imagines. The British public has proved remarkably reluctant to give up using real money. Over the past decade, the total value of bank notes in circulation has doubled to £40 billion. On top of that there is another £3.5 billion worth of coins in circulation. These are astounding quantities. It suggests that every man, woman, and child in Britain has over £700 stashed away in notes and coins. There certainly isn't much of it in my wallet, and I don't believe quite that much can have slipped from our pockets and sucked into the impenetrable upholstery of our sofas. So someone, somewhere, is hoarding an awful lot of cash—and making the decision that they are better off doing that than they are earning some interest in a bank.

Why do they do it? I don't believe it is just a desire to escape the taxman. There is something about the world of bank accounts and credit cards that is deeply disturbing. I hate it when I try to buy something online or over the telephone, and the computer or sales assistant seems to know my financial history. But more to the point, credit cards and debit cards are a gift to fraudsters. In 2005/06, Britons were defrauded via their credit cards to the tune of £430 million, a threefold increase over the past decade. Online fraud doubled to £23.2 million and telephone and mail order fraud increased by 21 percent to £183 million. In all, according to the European Security Transportation Association, one in five UK bank customers have had money stolen from them or fallen victim to scams involving their credit cards.

A typical victim was Steve, whose identity was stolen when he moved house. An unsolicited invitation to take out a credit card was intercepted by thieves, who filled out the application form in his name and proceeded to run up £4,400 of debt. Steve found out about the fraud when he applied to increase the credit limit on his—genuine—credit card, and was denied credit. Not only did his own bank hold him responsible for the fraud; the information was instantly shared with other banks, making it difficult for him to obtain credit anywhere. Two-and-a-half years and a lot of hassle later, he finally managed to convince his bank that he had nothing to do with the £4,400 spent in his name.

Steve was lucky. According to the European Commission, 31 percent of Britons who have been defrauded via their credit cards are never reimbursed by their banks, the banks arguing that they bore some responsibility for the fraud by being careless with their cards or PINs. If we are going to be held responsible for money that is spirited out of our bank accounts, where we put it for safekeeping, imagining that it would be kept in some virtual strong-room, why put it in banks at all?

It is bizarre that electronic money should be less secure than its physical equivalent. If someone bashes us over the head in a dark alleyway and steals our wallet, we accept it is going to be hard to trace, but surely if someone steals money via a credit card there is going to be a data trail leading straight to the door of the thief. So why does it seem so hard for the law to catch up with fraudsters? On the one hand, credit cards are being used to amass vast quantities of personal data on our lifestyle and shopping habits—information that is then used to carpet-bomb us with junk mail and target us with cold calls from marketing organizations. On the other hand, when we are defrauded, the data trail seems to stop short of the culprits.

At least Steve managed to obtain a crime report from the police, which helped him reclaim money from the bank. Overall, however, the reaction of law enforcers to credit card fraud is one of astonishing indifference. In April 2007, the Home Office decided that credit card customers who discover that they have been defrauded should no longer contact the police, only their bank. The bank will then be free to decide whether or not to report the fraud to the police. In other words, credit card fraud has effectively ceased to be treated as a criminal offense. Instead, it is being treated as an occupational hazard for card-holders and bankers: they shouldn't expect to get their money back, only to insure themselves against their losses. Big Brother may be watching you, but he doesn't seem to be terribly bothered about watching your wallet.

It is certainly not a shortage of computing power that prevents the forces of law and order from tracing the fraudsters. Should I make an international transaction, it will end up being recorded in the bowels of a computer in Belgium, to which the CIA has access. The Belgian-based Society for Worldwide Interbank Financial Telecommunication (SWIFT) is a co-operative which daily handles $6 trillion worth of international cash transfers on behalf of 7,800 banks. After 9/11, US officials realized the potential of this data for tracing movements of cash by terrorist groups, and persuaded SWIFT to allow the CIA to rummage through the data—at first with few restrictions. It was only in 2003, when SWIFT became worried what its customers would think if they discovered intimate details of their financial transactions were being studied by the CIA, that restrictions on use of the data were imposed—the CIA is now supposed to keep records of all searches it makes on the database, justifying each one and not embarking on "fishing" expeditions to trawl through the data in search of petty offenders.

It would be wrong to condemn the use of SWIFT's data by anti-terrorism officers, when it is clear that terrorists can be caught in this way: the US claims to have traced the mastermind behind the 2002 al-Qaeda bombings in Bali using SWIFT data. It would just be nice if our government's use of financial data wasn't so secretive. It says something of the US's enthusiasm for accessing the data that the US would rather we didn't know what it was up to. When the *New York Times* wrote of the use of SWIFT data in 2006, government officials several times attempted to persuade the newspaper not to run the story.

I certainly wouldn't like to be without a debit card. It is easy to forget the sheer tedium of obtaining money abroad before credit and debit cards: the long search for a bank, followed by the drawn-out business of cashing in a traveler's check. Nowadays, one simply stuffs a card in a machine, from Mumbai to Marrakesh, and out pops some local currency. But the trade-off for the convenience is that we are at the mercy of vast impersonal systems which we don't understand, and, should we be defrauded or fall victim to an error, we can be completely screwed. In the world of electronic transactions, you are absolutely nobody without a credit history. Or a postcode. Recently, the Post Office decided to change my postcode, which has led to my card being rejected because the address I have given doesn't tally with that registered on the card. From such simple things like that, horrible inconvenience can result. How I wished for a lovely big wad of cash then.

The masters of our financial status are credit agencies, which gather information on our financial conduct and sell the information on to subscribing commercial organizations who want to check our creditworthiness. Get a lousy credit rating—sometimes through no fault of your own - and you can wave goodbye to that new car.

A citizen has the right to see his "credit file," and to complain if any of the information on it is inaccurate. Good job, too. According to a 2007 survey by the consumer association Which?, one in five people who have asked to see their credit files have discovered errors in the information held on them by credit agencies.

The rub is that somebody is doing very nicely out of granting you the privilege of showing you your credit file. You can, for example, obtain the information from a website called www.checkmyfile.com, run by a company called the Credit Reporting Agency Ltd in Truro, Cornwall. How much did this bunch know about me? All would be revealed, read the boilerplate, in return for the sum of £16.95. Somewhat reluctantly, I paid. In return I was granted access to—selective—parts of my "credit files" held by the three credit agencies operating in the UK: Experian, Equifax, and Callcredit.

Experian seemed a little shy in revealing information that it held about me. It told me that I had been on the electoral roll since 1999 (perfectly true), that I am not bankrupt, that I have no county court judgments against my name and that CIFAS, a fraud prevention operation, has no file on me. Equifax was a little more forthcoming, telling me the names of everyone registered as being on the electoral roll at my property since *1984*. It told me that I was up to date on payments on my credit cards—and the size of my credit limit. My mouth dropped open as it then told me the size of my mortgage, and proudly informed me that such information was shared with 250 lenders, utility companies, and other commercial concerns.

It also revealed how many commercial organizations had conducted searches (i.e., had a peep at my finances) against my name in the past year. It was zero. If it struck me as reassuring that nobody had been spying on my bank accounts, I was soon put right: "Up to about 10 searches a year is perfectly normal. Very low levels of searches can tell lenders that you are not very credit active, so they may be not so willing to lend to you." In other words, they aren't going to advance me any money, not because they are worried I won't repay my debts, but out of fear that I will repay them too soon, without their having a chance to ensnare me in debt at high rates of interest.

I could find out a little bit more, it turned out, by going to the credit agencies directly—and handing over even more cash. Experian, for example, invited me to keep a constant eye on my credit file for the sum of £5.99 a month. In return, the boilerplate reassured me, I would be able to find out whether a fraudster had stolen my identity. Their file on me recorded the credit limit on my credit card, the size of my mortgage and monthly repayments, and whether I was up to date with my repayments. It also told me the identity of any organizations that had checked my creditworthiness over the past few months. Until the law was changed to make it illegal for credit agencies to divulge third-party information, it seems I could also have found out these financial details for anyone else living at my address.

The one thing that none of the credit agencies would tell me, and by implication won't tell other subscribers to their service, was the size of my bank balance. At present, it so happens, it is not legal for banks to reveal the size of our bank balances to credit agencies. But I wouldn't be so sure that this happy state of affairs will continue. Having revealed intimate details of my finances, Checkmyfile.com then flashed up on my computer screen the chance to sign a petition appealing to the government not to allow banks to disseminate this very information—which Checkmyfile believed "would drive a coach and horses through banking confidentiality, the data protection acts and our human right to privacy."

It is bizarre to think that the government is planning to let credit agencies advertise the contents of our bank accounts—yet will not allow police forces to name convicted criminals. In March 2007, Suffolk police put out a warning to householders to protect themselves against three prolific burglars who were about to be released from jail on parole. The warning missed out, however, one vital element: the burglars' names. Police withheld this information—for fear of "violating the individuals' privacy."

Come to think of it, why do the banks need a new law to exchange details of our bank accounts with each other, when they have already found a method of sharing the information with the general public—or, to be more precise, anyone prepared to rummage through their rubbish bins? In March 2007, the Information Commissioner revealed that 12 banks had been caught dumping intimate details of their customers' bank accounts in waste bins. Included were credit card application forms revealing personal details, a mortgage application along with the customer's bank statements, and some papers which revealed a customer's PIN.

Coming next: a law obliging us to write our bank balances on our shirtfronts, along with a large arrow pointing to the pocket in which we keep our wallets—to help the country's anonymous band of thieves go about their work without fear of having their privacy infringed by being caught.

CHAPTER FIFTEEN

ME AND MY SHOPPING

"We do not accept junk mail."

— Notice on recycling bin in local authority waste-disposal unit.

I'm glad my local supermarket is not close to the campus of Eastern Kentucky University. If it was I could expect to find a pimply youth or two lurking the other side of the ice cream freezer, furtively scribbling down whether I had opted for raspberry ripple or plain vanilla. To quote an assignment from the university's course on marketing:

> Choose some person (must be a stranger) shopping in a supermarket and observe that person from the time they enter the parking lot until they leave the store. Be sure the subject is not aware that you are observing him/her. Take a tablet and a pen or pencil with you so that you can make a list of items purchased.

It is an unsophisticated introduction to marketing techniques. It has overtones, in fact, of Mass Observation, the body of volunteers assembled by British sociologist Tom Harrisson in the 1930s to observe the habits of the general public. To quote but one nugget from one of his works, *The Pub and the People*, in which his volunteers cowered in the corner of pubs in Bolton, "the percentage of men wearing caps drops from 69.4 on Sunday to 58.8 on Saturday."

Real, qualified marketing people of course do not hover around the vegetable counter in raincoats, with their collars turned up. They do not need to. The gathering of information on our shopping habits has come on leaps and bounds since those modest beginnings in the 1930s. It has become a huge, unseen industry.

In George Orwell's *1984*, Winston Smith was rudely interrupted during his morning exercises by a voice from his television screen telling him to put in more effort. It could have been worse. He could have had a supermarket loyalty card. Then he would have been woken up every so often by an envelope full of vouchers imploring him to buy more greens.

So far, this book has concentrated on the collection and use of data by the state. But of course commercial organizations are at it too. A modern supermarket is a ruthlessly efficient machine for collecting data on everything we buy, down to the last cabbage. Unless you make a habit of always paying by cash, your shopping habits will have been meticulously logged in the dastardly shop's computer, traced to you by your credit card. Take out a loyalty card and the potential for collecting data on your grocery habits becomes even greater. Every pomegranate, every whisky bottle, every part-baked toad-in-the-hole will be registered in a great personal shopping file on a mainframe, where it will be analyzed, regurgitated and used to hector you into buying more of the sort of thing that it feels your sort of people ought to be buying.

It's all about to get a lot cleverer, too. At present, all that shops have to distinguish between different goods is a barcode. This can be scanned at the point of sale and each can of parsnip soup linked to your credit card or loyalty card. If you purchase the product with cash, on the other hand, your parsnip soup habit escapes detection. But imagine if each soup tin were to be fitted with a small transmitter which constantly broadcast its whereabouts? Each tin could transmit a signal to the till as it was wheeled through the checkout, allowing the cash register automatically to tot up your purchases and bill you accordingly—making checkout staff, and queues, redundant. It could also tell if you had walked out of the shop without paying for your soup—allowing the fuzz to pursue you all the way home to your pantry.

Not only that: clothes shops could instantly tell if you had walked into a shop with a skirt sold by a rival outlet, concealed in a bag, and then sniffed at the opportunity to buy a top to go with the skirt. In fact, my publishers could fit this book with such a device and tell exactly who had bought this book, to whom they had passed it on, where it was being read, and—shame—trace anyone who dared dispose of it.

This is not science fiction. The device which allows shops to do all these things already exists. It is called a Radio Frequency Identification (RFID) tag, and is already fitted to some products. In 2003, it was revealed that anyone picking up a pack of Gillette Mach 3 razor blades at a Tesco supermarket in Cambridge was triggering a camera. The shop had suffered the attentions of a razor blade thief and was hoping to catch him.

The only thing which so far has prevented RFIDs from becoming ubiquitous is that at present they cost too much money—about five pence each—to be commercially viable. When the cost comes down to a penny or so, there will be an explosion in their use. You won't be able to tell that this has happened (experts predict it will be around 2010) because an RFID—at least the simpler, "passive" version of the device—is about the size of a pinhead. The passive version, at present, can only be read over distances of a few feet, although that may of course change. So, if you want to avoid leaving a data trail of your shopping habits from one end of the High Street to the other and back home to your wardrobe or pantry—shopping is going to involve the painstaking business of seeking out the bug on every item you buy and ripping it off.

Even Winston Smith was not accosted by his breakfast. But how much longer before our cereal packets, like the lamp-posts, start to speak to us? One company has developed "flat cardboard speakers," which can be incorporated into a cardboard box and programmed to spout forth special offers. Or, for that matter, healthy eating advice. If there is one nightmare which Orwell failed to foresee it is the voice of the health minister lecturing us for taking one helping of Frosted Flakes too many.

I don't know whether to be spooked or not by this vast private espionage on our shopping and eating habits. The relaxed view is that all the nosey supermarkets are trying to do is sell us more bagels and soap powder. It's not as if Tesco operatives are going to follow us home and nag us on the doorstep for not buying this week's special offer doughnuts.

On the other hand, there is potentially a darker side. You may be unaware of what happens to the data that is collected by commercial organizations. Details of your shopping habits are used, either directly or by being sold on to other marketing organizations, to build a picture of you and your neighborhood, so that they can better target you with the type of junk mail to which they think your demographic category will respond. You wonder how 5.1 billion items of junk mail found their way through British letter boxes last year? It is little comfort to know that they got there by precision bombing rather than carpet-bombing. When the junk-mailers sent you that special offer for flowery sofa cushions it was because they knew that people in your postcode district have a soft spot for that sort of thing. (Though not all marketing organizations use the data effectively. According to the credit agency Equifax, 22 million items of junk mail every year are addressed and sent to the deceased.)

Little known to most British citizens, we have all been classified, like the squashed specimens in some Victorian naturalist's scrapbook, into species and sub-species. One of the most-used classifications is the Mosaic system devised by Experian, a credit agency and information company which grew out of Great Universal Stores (in the US, Axiom provides a similar product). It divides Britain into 11 groups and 61 "lifestyle" subgroups, according to postcodes. Experian tell me that I am in a group called "Symbols of Success," subgroup "Semi-Rural Seclusion." When I read the description I blush with self-satisfaction. Apparently I am a "wealthy, independent, and contented" person who has "made very deliberate choices to live a life that marries the modern world with more traditional values and pursuits." Not only that: I am confident of my judgment and "well integrated into the community." Oh, and my garden "is likely to be planted with cherry trees." (Spookily, it is.)

While I loll about in this Chekovian world, others are not so fortunate. I am not sure how I would take to being categorized as one of the "Bedsit Beneficiaries," who live in "the heartland of the large sliced white loaf," leading "particularly passive lives" and "failing to take responsibility for their futures." Actually, on second thought, reading the description it sounds as if I would be well past caring what Experian thought of me.

Even so it could be worse: I could be of the group entitled "Families on Benefits," who are "poorly educated young parents for whom bringing up their children is a constant struggle" and whose areas are pervaded by a "mood of fatalism and aimless indirection." Ouch!

Does it matter if that is how advertisers think of you? Well, there are some relatively trivial disadvantages. For a start, down at this level, you spend a lot longer hanging on the phone listening to synthesized Vivaldi: call centers now use systems that rank callers according to their spending power, so that big-spending individuals are shunted up the queue ahead of Bedsit Beneficiaries, and indeed above tight-fisted scrooges like me. Worse, living on the wrong side of the tracks makes it hard to get credit. And if you can't get a mortgage, how are you going to get out of your low-life postcode and rid yourself of your fatalism and indirection?

The postcode analysis used by commercial organizations is playing its part in institutionalizing an urban underclass. Besides being trapped by the benefit system—which can penalize the poor if they start to earn—people are being written off as commercial no-hopers, thanks to the economic habits of the people whom they live amongst. That isn't exactly helping to create what the government calls "balanced communities."

The traditional market was a place of joy, with a constructive tension between seller and buyer setting the prices and ensuring the quality. No one can say that our modern retail chains are not responsive to customer demand—they have analyzed it from every angle possible. But still it feels like a cold world where every purchase you make is stored in some distant Lubyanka, and used to manipulate your next shopping trip. I think I might get an allotment just to get the retailers off my back. Even then, I wouldn't bet against Tesco spotting it on Google Earth and sending me vouchers for carrots at half the price I am paying for seeds.

CHAPTER SIXTEEN

ME AND MY JOB

"Calls may be recorded for staff-training purposes."

— Ubiquitous message which really means: congratulations, you have
just consented to being spied upon by the company you have telephoned.

I always wonder what staff "training" is on the dozen or so times a day I
hear the above message. I imagine it to be something like one of Stalin's
re-education camps, where unclean thoughts are washed from the brains
of errant telemarketing staff. Indeed, employees' unclean thoughts appear
to be a popular target for companies in Britain and America.

The 23 staffers at the *New York Times'* shared services center in Norfolk, Virginia never saw it coming. Their work processing payments for the
company's staff was so routine that they had taken to enlivening dull after-
noons by sending each other smutty jokes, pornography, and jokes about
their bosses. What they didn't realize, this being the early days of internet
and email, was that everything they did was being watched. And before
long, the bosses pounced. The company didn't exactly specify which of the
transgressions was most heinous, but they sacked the staff for violation of
its email policy—and for fear that the offensive emails could form the basis
of expensive harassment cases.

This was 1999, and the dismissed individuals had just become the first
victims of a crackdown on staff who abused the company's email system,

on which any personal communication was forbidden. At the time, few workers understood that emails would remain on the hard disks of their computers long after they thought they had "deleted" them.

Since 1999, snooping on staff has become endemic. Never mind the right to privacy which was supposedly enshrined within the Human Rights Act: few employers are likely to be caught acting outside the law when they listen in on the telephone conversations of their staff or intercept their emails. Although under the Regulation of Investigatory Powers Act of 2000, employers are supposed to obtain their employees' consent to be snooped upon, in practice this is easily obtained by the simple expedient of putting a clause in the employment contract. In any case, the Telecommunications (Lawful Business Practices) (Interpretation of Communications) Regulations of 2000 gives employers the right to monitor and record their employees' telephone conversations and emails without consent if the purpose is to detect criminal activity.

Personally, workplace surveillance is something of a foreign world to me. I have not had a proper job in 20 years—unless you count the day I spent picking strawberries on a Kentish farm in the late 1980s, after which I resigned in sympathy with a colleague who had been spotted talking (God knows what would have happened had they spotted one of us popping a strawberry into our mouth—gassing?). I don't have to fear the humiliation faced by most employees: a call to the boss's office, followed by a few minutes' opportunity to stuff my kids' photographs in a black trash bag before being escorted from the premises. I don't know what it is like to receive a smutty email from a friend at work, and look over my shoulder, trembling to see whether the boss is around, before sloping off to ask a colleague in systems how long, you know, information is stored on the office computers...

Nor is it just office computers. Increasingly staff whose work involves driving are finding out that their every movement can be monitored by their boss—so that a lunch hour of 61 minutes may be noted, as well as the time they were driving the company car and "got caught in slow traffic" in the back streets of King's Cross (honest, chief). Employers have been known to hire private investigators to check for staff on sick leave who nevertheless manage to make it to the golf course, and even to pry into the drinking and smoking habits of staff off-duty.

Surveillance of employees isn't entirely a recent phenomenon—one thinks of the sinister "time and motion" men of the 1960s who lurked around the office bathroom measuring how long employees were spending away from their desks. But at least in those days it had never occurred to bosses to fit soap dispensers with sensors to check that their grubbier employers were using enough soap, or fit covert CCTV in the rest room, a practice that was banned in the US and under New South Wales' Workplace Surveillance Act (2005).

Perhaps the rise in workplace surveillance is best understood as a simple response to the technology as it becomes available. Back in the 1980s, bosses didn't tend to rummage through employees' waste paper bins for smutty notes passed around the office. Only when email became common did rude and offensive office exchanges become such an issue. Why do firms scan computer hard disks for incriminating information? Because they can.

Likewise, employees on the road used to be able to get away with all sorts. Then came the Global Positioning System (GPS). Should we be worried that our employers want to follow our movements? Not according to Tim Hibbard, software developer for an American company called EnGraph, which sells software packages to distribution companies wanting to track their staff and vehicles. He is so convinced of the good of the technology that he has set up a website, www.timhibbard.com/wherestim, which tracks his own whereabouts constantly for the benefit of fellow nerds everywhere, and plots it on Google Earth.

I became quite intrigued following Tim on his travels around the Midwest. In fact, I almost feel I know the guy. He seems to spend an awful lot of time on a half-completed housing estate off East 1000th Road in Lawrence, Kansas, quite possibly because he lives there. But even more fascinating are his travels—which anyone can follow in real time—and at real speed. It is the precise nature of the information that particularly impresses—and the chilling realization that had I a job as a traveling salesman, that could be me.

When I logged on one Sunday, Tim was heading west on Interstate 35 just outside Des Moines, Iowa—at 54 mph. My first reaction was to email his co-ordinates to US bomber command. But then, as his speed crept up to 78 mph, an even more dastardly plan occurred to me. I checked the speed limit on Iowa's interstates—which turned out to be 70 mph—then emailed Iowa State Patrol Division, just to ask them politely whether they were interested. I got a very nice reply from the splendidly-named Sergeant Genie Clemens, the patrol's Safety Education Coordinator: "We would not use this kind of evidence to issue a citation. However it is very fascinating equipment. Thanks for the information!" I think if I were Tim Hibbard and intent on informing the world about my travels I might just ease off a little on the gas.

I would sooner work for Tim, though, than for Cincinnati-based security firm Citywatcher.com. In 2006, three workers agreed to have radio frequency identification tags (RFIDs) implanted in their arms to allow them automatic entry to highly secure parts of the firm's premises. To show solidarity with the employees, the company's chief executive officer Sean Darks decided that he would have one implanted himself, telling reporters, "I'm not going to ask somebody to do something I wouldn't do myself."

That is very noble of him. But still I wonder whether he has really thought it through. If you want to barcode yourself like a can of soup on a supermarket shelf, you shouldn't be surprised to be treated like one. I wouldn't be at all surprised if every time he walked through a supermarket checkout he got charged for his arm.

And what if he decides to sack one of his bionic employees? Normally, this is a fairly simple business involving the confiscation of his security pass. But if Mr. Darks sacks one of his three chipped employees, he will presumably have to have him wheeled down to the nearest hospital, held down, and anaesthetized while his radio tag is surgically removed. Otherwise, every time the spurned employee walks past the office, security doors will be flung open to the world.

It is not just offices. In 2005, Brittan Elementary School in Sutter, California became the first in the world to force its pupils to wear RFID tags in order to track their whereabouts in the school. The technology is claimed to have made redundant the tedious business of teachers taking attendance—the presence of pupils is automatically recorded as soon as they walk through the classroom door. One thing, however, does not appear to have occurred to the authorities: that crafty children might take it in turns to take each other's RFID tags to lessons: e.g., "I'll take your RFID to geography if you take mine to math." Only a pair of identical twins can fool a teacher who takes note of who is present by a mixture of attendance-calling and visual identification; but with a dumb RFID scanner it's pretty easy to skip lessons—unless the school is going to staple the RFIDs, as with livestock, to pupils' ears. On balance, if I were running a school, I think I would stop trying to treat kids like cattle and just try to make the lessons more interesting.

There are also schools that use fingerprinting to identify pupils and teachers. One has to feel sorry for poor Kenneth Payne, a trained teacher in California who can't get a job. Why not? Because he suffers from a condition called atopic dermatitis, which causes the skin on his fingertips to peel, making it impossible for him to give a fingerprint. As a result, he can't fulfill the rules requiring every teacher in California to give their fingerprints—and so cannot work in a school. Even Kafka couldn't have come up with a more poignant tale.

The more I read about workplace surveillance, the more pleased I am to have made my escape from the world of employment. If employees do a good job, so what if they want to snigger at the odd smutty email? The surveillance of their every move is like some bizarre protestant ritual based on the belief that work is a punishment for our sins and should be tedious, preferably unpleasant, at every turn. One would think that employers were grown-up enough nowadays to judge workers on results, not on some rude email they sent to Sandra in Accounting three weeks ago.

Not that the existence of workplace surveillance has exactly stopped employees misusing their computers: according to a recent study by Dr. Monica Whitty, a psychologist at Queens University, Belfast, 40 percent of British workers still use their email for office gossip and seven percent still take the risk of downloading pornography at work. I suspect a good few employers would love to examine their employees' hard disks, but dare not for fear that if they actually started implementing their policies against misuse of office computers they wouldn't have a workforce left.

The one good thing about the rise in workplace surveillance is that just occasionally it backfires on the boss, big-time. I would love to have been slaving away at the coalface of the US healthcare company whose chief executive one morning in 2001 wrote a fiery email to staff complaining that they were only working 40 hours a week, and that he wanted to see the car park full in the early mornings, late evenings, and on the weekends.

Disgruntled employees quickly forwarded the email to just about everyone they could think of—with the result that, once the world knew what a bastard the boss was, the company's shares plunged by 30 percent the next day.

CHAPTER SEVENTEEN

ME AND MY HEALTH

"Totally F***ed but unfortunately not dead yet"

– The meaning of the acronym TFBUNDY found on a patient's medical notes.

First the good part. All patients in Britain's National Health Service (NHS) now have the right to see their medical notes. That means—theoretically at least—that no doctor will any longer risk writing rude statements about you. Unless of course he takes the trouble to disguise them as acronyms like the one above, or like FODTTFO (Fell over drunk, told to f*** off), NFN (Normal for Norfolk) and GROLIES (Guardian reader of limited intelligence in ethnic skirt).

The flipside to this greater openness for patients is that others, too, have gained much greater freedom to nose around your medical notes. Until recently, you could more or less be assured of complete discretion from your GP, whether your problem was an itchy backside or a sexual preference for tractors. No longer, though, can you be sure that the details of your embarrassing problem will remain under lock-and-key in a filing cabinet at the doctor's office: the government has decided that henceforth all medical records should be entered onto a computer database called Connecting for Health, to which doctors and nurses all over the country will have access. You may even get to see your medical notes online—a hundred GPs' practices have begun experimenting with a scheme that allows patients to view their own medical records on a website with the use of a password. The system was first tried as a means of boosting confidence in the medical profession for the surviving patients of Dr. Harold Shipman, the Greater Manchester GP who managed to bump off two hundred of his elderly patients before being caught.

There is a valid rationale for putting medical notes online: if you end up unconscious and requiring urgent medical treatment, you don't want doctors trying to get through to your surgery to find out whether you suffer from any allergies before administering treatment. As former Prime Minister Tony Blair said when selling the project to the nation: "If I live in Bradford and fall ill in Birmingham I want the NHS to be able to treat me."

Yet Connecting for Health has been a disaster in more ways than one. Its cost has already risen to three times its original £6.2 billion budget. Moreover, doctors' attempts to book hospital appointments for their patients using the system has all too often ended in failure. But equally worrying is the potential for misuse of personal data held on the computer system. How do we know that intimate details of our hemorrhoids will not end up being broadcast unto the nation? We don't. In fact, the evidence so far suggests that this is exactly what will happen. In April 2007, the NHS Medical Training Application Service (MTAS) website went haywire and decided to advertise the addresses, telephone numbers, and qualifications of hundreds of junior doctors to any member of the public who visited the site—along with details of their religion, sexual orientation, and any police record.

And that slip-up was entirely self-inflicted. Once hackers rise to the challenge, as they inevitably will, gaping holes in the system will be exposed.

There is also the question of the accuracy of information that finds its way onto Connecting for Health. The Royal Academy of Engineering reports the case of an NHS practice manager who discovered that her medical records recorded that she was a penitent at an alcoholism clinic—a complete surprise to her. The misrepresentation occurred, apparently, when her medical records were spinning around the NHS computer systems.

But the greatest achievement of the MTAS has been to recruit at least half a dozen al-Qaeda terror suspects. The failed terror attacks in London and Glasgow in July 2007 resulted in the arrest of six NHS doctors, one of whose reading of the Hippocratic Oath led him to drive into the crowded terminal building at Glasgow Airport in a jeep laden with explosives and gas canisters. One appreciates that al-Qaeda trains its recruits to lead quiet, diligent lives so as not to arouse suspicion—and therefore it might not be easy to spot the odd rogue hematologist whose real interest in blood is to spill it. But you'd expect hospitals to be in control of their job interviews—which are vital for weeding out candidates who have lied about their qualifications or are slightly shifty about their motives for wanting the job. Astonishingly, however, hospitals are told which candidates to interview according to how the candidates fill in a computerized application form—a form that only gives 25 percent of the score for qualifications and 75 percent for 150-word answers on general issues such as ethics. This clearly favors those who can spin a good spiel over those with a genuine ability to do the job.

While MTAS can check British applicants for criminal records, it cannot vet foreign applicants to the same extent—and so cannot detect whether an applicant has spent six months in a terrorist training camp in Afghanistan. Not for the first time, an automated system that gives the impression of tight surveillance turns out to be a good deal less safe than the system it replaced.

But for me, the biggest worry about Connecting for Health is that it appears to be shifting the ethos of medicine from treating illness to a system that monitors and treats us whether we are ill or not. Until quite recently, the personal relationship between you and your doctor was an important part of medicine. Your doctor got to understand your quirks, and could work out quite easily whether you really had suffered the heart attack and had contracted the bowel cancer you said you had, or whether you were just suffering from a touch of hypochondria. We are moving, however, to a system based on mass collection and processing of data, where such subtleties are less likely to be detected.

Take the NHS program to get a huge proportion of the population on statins, the cholesterol-lowering drugs. Patients over 40 have been assessed for their supposed chances of developing heart disease, and 4.7 million of them have been told that they are at risk. This huge operation has resulted in the NHS running up an annual bill of £2 billion to prescribe the drugs.

Yet the patients haven't really been diagnosed at all. They have been picked out for statins not because they are ill, but because their lifestyle and socio-economic status identifies them as a statistical risk.

While the nation nervously pops pills and waits to be struck down by a heart attack, a team writing in the *British Medical Journal* reassessed the evidence and concluded that the methodology was wrong: in fact only 3.2 million people are really at sufficient risk from developing heart disease to justify the prescription of statins. In other words, 1.5 million people have been put on the drugs, and made to worry, for no reason at all—other than to help the NHS to reach a target.

Mercifully, the NHS is a long way behind many other countries, and private health companies, when it comes to mass screening programs. I could, for example, book in for a CT (computerized tomography) scan at one of the clinics advertising on the internet with soft-focus pictures of scanners and potted plants. CT scanning is the medical equivalent of Northampton town center. "We are able to view your heart, lungs and colon with such precision that we can provide you with peace of mind and spot early signs of diseases before it is too late," goes the reassuring pitch.

I don't know about you, but I don't want to have my ticker monitored like some piece of industrial plant. Okay, I am going to be struck down by something at some point, but until then can't I just enjoy being well, without knowing there is some pimple deep in my insides which one day might just grow into something nasty? As one critic from within the medical world puts it: "If you are going to have your body scanned for abnormalities, virtually everyone is going to find some, but the worry and distress outweighs any advantage." A lot of cancers just disappear of their own accord, without the patient ever knowing they had them—unless of course they have paid several hundred pounds to have their body wrung through a CT scanner. With screening, the concept of good health is virtually abolished: everyone is in remission from something or other.

It is easy to sell the benefits of comprehensive medical screening. You just quote cancer survival rates, which are usually higher in countries with large amounts of medical screening than in countries without. In the UK, for example, 35.9 percent of men survive for at least five years after being diagnosed with the most common forms of cancer, compared with 44.6 percent in France and 44.7 percent in Germany. But it is a mirage. If screening really did save lives you would expect life expectancy to be lower in the UK than in France and Germany, but it isn't. British men live to an average of 76.1 years, exactly the same as in France and only two months less than in Germany. The reason cancer survival rates are higher in France and Germany is that cancers are being detected earlier. British men suffering from cancer may die quicker after diagnosis, but they don't necessarily die at an earlier age.

Consider where this obsessive medical screening could lead if we allow it to: monitors being implanted inside our bodies to keep us under constant medical surveillance. You think it is a joke? In April 2007, Malcolm Wicks, the British science minister, floated the idea that the elderly and confused might have microchips inserted under their skin so that they can go out shopping on their own, and yet easily be returned should they forget where they are—or indeed who they are. Should they be found wandering the High Street, no longer will passers-by have to take at face value their protestation that they are King Richard III. They would be able to call a policeman who would scan the microchip under their arm and conclusively say, "no, this is not Richard III, it is Arthur Muggins of number 3 Cherry Tree Court, Bognor Regis."

Already 18 diabetics in the US have been implanted with microchips to monitor their glucose levels; around 70 Americans have agreed to have themselves implanted with RFIDs to help doctors identify them if they become confused and to gain instant access to their medical records. One of them is Retired Lt. Commander Daniel Hickey, who had a chip inserted in his upper arm at the suggestion of his doctors, saying, "I didn't mull over it or anything. It just makes a lot of sense to me."

Lt. Commander Hickey is a satisfied customer of a US company called VeriChip, which markets RFIDs for all kinds of purposes, from workplace security systems to parents who want to keep track of their children. The company's case is that by implanting patients with RFIDs it could help reduce the 98,000 deaths in the US every year caused by medical errors. As Joseph Feldman, MD, Chairman of Emergency Medicine at Hackensack University Medical Center explains: "Trying to identify unidentified patients is torture. You go through pockets, computer records and make phone calls. It can take well over an hour."

Dr. Feldman is possibly right. Implanting everyone with a RFID chip might save lives (notwithstanding the possibility that if done in Britain Connecting for Health might mistakenly link you up with the medical records of a maniac, and have you sedated). But the idea of being implanted with a chip still does not appeal to me. One hates to think of the consequences should we all be treated like Royal Mail parcels with a digitized postcode. Judging by the number of times I have had post delivered to me in Cambridge that has apparently gone via Cardiff or Carlisle, I think there is a strong possibility, should I suffer a head injury, of being dispatched for treatment to the chiropody clinic.

Once the NHS has its vast database of health records up and running, accessible via microchips implanted in patients' arms, you can be pretty sure that it won't just be doctors who have access to it. Won't employers demand access, too, so they can check that we aren't lying on our CV when we say we are in good health? Maybe restaurants, too, wary of being sued, will demand to check that we aren't suffering from cardiac disease before they serve us that double helping of gateau.

And don't let us even get started on how the supermarkets would love to use the information. Wheel your trolley down the vegetable aisle and I can just hear the words ringing in my ear: "You are just passing the carrots. Carrots are high in vitamin A, which would be just ideal for your heart condition..."

CHAPTER EIGHTEEN

ME AND MY PARANOIA

"Worried what your partner is up to? Why not give them one of our spyphones with any of our special features installed as a gift for their birthday or a special occasion? Whatever they are keeping from you, you will know about it."

— Advertisement on website selling covert surveillance equipment.

And who said romance is dead? There you were, thinking of fobbing her off with a box of Godiva chocolates when instead you could be setting her up with a phone which will allow you to trace the weekly visits you suspect she is making to Reginald's house.

When we use the term "surveillance society" we tend to mean surveillance carried out by, or on behalf of, public authorities or commercial organizations. But there is another, growing side to surveillance: the public spying on each other, either by amateur sleuthing or via the private espionage industry. The man sitting in the nondescript car parked outside your house tapping away at his laptop and secretly intercepting your telephone calls and emails is less visible than the police cars on our streets, but he and his eavesdropping colleagues are a good deal more numerous. According to the Security Industry Authority (SIA), set up by the government in 2001 to regulate private eyes, bouncers, wheel-clampers, and other such workers, there are 500,000 private "security operatives" in business in Britain—outnumbering the nation's 136,000 police officers more than three to one. The industry, it calculates, has an annual turnover of £3-£4 billion.

Not that the SIA sees this, in itself, as a problem. Far from it. Rather the SIA believes "that a professional, regulated, private security industry has the potential to become a valuable member of the extended police family." What a wonderful expression, "the extended police family." It is worthy, in fact, of the Stasi itself. How much longer before most of the population has been co-opted into the secret services?

In March 2006, the government recognized the growing menace of private surveillance by introducing a licensing system for private security staff. Since that date it has been necessary for bouncers, private security guards, and private eyes first to undertake 20 hours of training and then to apply for a license, at a cost of £245—a little plastic laminated card that they must wear when on duty. Working without a license can cost a private security guard a stiff fine. Whether it is especially reassuring to the public to see a security guard wearing one of these cards is another matter. The SIA's website reassures applicants that a criminal record will not necessarily disqualify them for a license. Indeed, if their conviction for "common assault and battery," "culpable and reckless injury," or "causing alarm or distress" is more than five years old, they will be approved.

On top of Britain's 500,000 security operatives is an unknown number of members of the public carrying out DIY surveillance. Where better to start spying on friends and family than with their mobile phone? A mobile is like a long silvery trail left by a slug. I dare say the slug—or phone-user—hardly notices, but it is there nonetheless. Your mobile phone company and any authority with which it is inclined to share the data has in its possession a record of your whereabouts. Or, more strictly perhaps, the whereabouts of your phone: were somebody in my case to take the data too literally they might conclude I have spent the past three years marooned up a Welsh mountain—the place where I lost my last phone.

So long as your phone is switched on it is constantly sending out and receiving signals to the nearest transmitter—sufficient to trace the location of the device to within 100 yards in urban areas, or a mile or so in rural areas. Rare is the crime nowadays that is solved without, somewhere along the line, involving data from a suspect's mobile phone. In 2002, law-enforcement bodies made 400,000 requests for data on individuals' use of their mobile phones.

But you don't have to be a policeman to track a mobile phone. Surf the internet and you can find numerous sites which allow private citizens to track mobile phones too. The service, needless to say, is advertised for its "good" uses, such as tracking the location of your own children. The website of one such service, which allows you to track a mobile phone of your choice for £180 a year, offers some wonderful idiots' advice: "Location services aimed at children are intended to compliment, but not to be a substitute for, normal parental supervision." I hadn't thought of that—fitting my kids with tracking devices and then disappearing for a few years until they turn 18.

I certainly wasn't going to turn down the opportunity to snoop on my own family. So, finding a service that offered a free 30-day trial, I signed up. It took five minutes. Then I had to wait 48 hours for my password to come through the post. After that, I simply tapped in the number of the mobile phone I wished to track and hey... I was transformed at a stroke into a spy.

There was just one little complication. The law insists that the users of phones being tracked must be warned of what is happening. When you wish to track a phone the device is sent a text message requesting that the user press a button confirming that he does not mind being tracked. All the same, there is no guarantee that it is really the user of the phone who replied to the text message—as opposed to somebody else who gained custody to it for a few minutes.

So, lifting my wife's mobile phone from her handbag, I replied to the text message, then slipped it back into her handbag. Next morning, an hour after she had driven off to the shops, I decided to track her down. The website professed to know exactly where she was: up came a map with a little brown figure supposedly marking the spot where she was. It wasn't the supermarket where she was meant to be—it was at a remote farmhouse five miles away. What was she doing there?

With images of her rolling around a haystack with a straw-haired farm-hand, I rang her phone to find out. And immediately... I heard my wife's mobile phone ringing from across the room. She had forgotten to take it with her. But for some reason the spying service thought the phone was five miles away. Curious, I decided to track my own mobile phone. That, too, was sitting in the room where I was. And yet the tracking service, too, decided that I was five miles away—on a riverbank.

The service, in other words, was not so much spooky as downright use-less. And to think I could have tracked her down, every afternoon, to the same remote farmhouse—and eventually turned up armed with a pitchfork to confront the yokel she was cavorting with.

Puzzled as to how a company could stay in business when its service was so bad, I tried the tracking service again several times, and found that the information was a lot more accurate when my wife ventured into urban areas. Mobile phone-tracking, I have since discovered, is the budget end of the private detection business. If I had wanted to delve more deeply, it wouldn't have been very difficult. To judge by the numerous websites vying to fulfill my surveillance needs, this is big business. For £299 I could buy a transmitter on the internet that was small enough to clip inside somebody's car or suitcase and track their whereabouts anywhere in the world—courtesy of the global positioning system, which utilizes 24 satellites launched by the US Department of Defense.

There is more to surveillance, of course, than simply knowing the where-abouts of your partner/business rival/stalking victim. What about listening in on their conversations? For £159 I could buy a "deleted text mes-sage reader," which, once plugged into the SIM card of my target's phone, would allow me to read "the messages they didn't want anyone to read." For £85 I could buy a phone-tapping device, small enough to slip into a telephone socket and capable of allowing me to listen to both sides of a conversation. Then there was a camera concealed inside a 7-Up can for £159, a smoke detector with a hidden night vision camera for £140. Or, if I want to listen to the neighbors (and I don't live in a tiny modern apartment with such thin walls I can hear them anyway) I could buy a "Listen through the wall device" for £189.

Never slow to spot a business opportunity, the same website also wanted to sell me, for £75, a "bug-detector" shaped like a pen, the end of which would flash whenever it detected the presence of a bug.

Does anyone really hate their spouse enough to buy this kind of stuff? They do indeed. According to the accountants Grant Thornton, 49 percent of all British court cases now involve the use of private detectives, typically hired at £200 a day. In the shadows of every suburban street, it seems, there stalks a private spook looking out for some private liaison. The irony is that divorce has become so easy nowadays that few people really need to catch their partner in flagrante in order to secure one, but for some reason they feel impelled to try nonetheless.

Is it really legal to tap into someone's phone? Well no, it isn't, if you do it without permission, as *News of the World* reporter Clive Goodman discovered at great expense in 2007, when he was jailed under the Regulation of Investigatory Powers Act of 2000 for tapping into the messaging services on Prince William's phone (result: a rather dull story that the prince had injured a tendon). But to judge by the amount of phone-tapping equipment for sale on the internet, it is a risk many are prepared to take. Neither is it legal to hack into the computer systems of telephone companies to obtain customers' telephone records—although you wouldn't think so from the many websites which mysteriously offer to sell you this data.

But there is plenty of spying—or rather let's call it information-gathering— which is perfectly legal. You can do quite a lot of spying from the comfort of your own computer. To start with, how about finding out where somebody lives? This is not a difficult task: every Briton over the age of 16 has, by law, to be entered on the electoral register. This, combined with the attainment of 18 years, allows them to vote—and also entitles them to receive mountains of junk mail, to be traced by old enemies and possibly to be stalked.

Until 2002, the Electoral Commission simply sold this information to whoever came up with the money. Then a pesky voter, fed up with junk mail, refused to sign the electoral register and threatened to take Britain to the European Court if, as a result, he was refused the right to vote. The government had second thoughts and introduced two versions of the register:

a "full" register and an "edited" register. Everyone has to be on the full register; which they do by filling in a form sent out by their local authority every autumn. The full register can be inspected in local council offices and can also be accessed by credit agencies for the purpose of checking the identity of people borrowing money or buying goods. Nosey citizens may not take copies of the full register, however: it is only to be used for the purpose of law enforcement.

The edited register is a different matter. You don't have to be on this version of the register. You can exclude yourself by checking a box on the form. There is a good reason for checking this box: the Electoral Commission flogs the information to anyone prepared to pay for it. Those who buy it include marketing companies and lots of websites that in turn sell it on to subscribers. Pay one of these companies £14.95 a month, or thereabouts, and you can quickly trace anyone to their home address. How many people realize this is tricky to say. I presumed that I must have checked the box, but no: when I looked myself up, there was my name and address.

The information on the edited version of the register, the Electoral Commission confirms, "can be used for any purpose." Presumably that includes assassination.

If I want to find the address and life history of an American citizen, it is even easier. I can visit a website called netsleuth.com and, in 10 minutes, obtain his driving license details, social security number, criminal history, details of any bankruptcy, and so on. "As silly as it sounds I really wanted to find my old high school sweetheart," says Rick of Branson, Michigan by way of a testimonial. "Unfortunately for me she is happily married, but it was still amazing that I found her in about 10 minutes." And she is presumably now cowering behind the sofa in fear of horrid, pimply Rick coming round to mess up her domestic bliss.

If my penchant for trailing and listening in on other members of the public is still not satisfied, even after deploying all the aforementioned kit, there is one more form of spying I can undertake. For just £29.95 I can buy my very own CCTV camera to mount on my home and spy on passers-by. It is perfectly legal, so long as I keep it trained on my property and warn passers-by with a little yellow triangular sign that says "surveillance in progress." In fact, the government seems quite keen for us to install CCTV equipment and all become mini Northampton town centers—although in an uncharacteristic failure to seize the initiative British authorities have not yet gone quite as far as Houston, Texas, where it may soon be illegal not to keep an eye on passers-by. The chief of police, Harold Hutt, has floated the idea that CCTV cameras should be a condition of planning permission for new housing.

Why do we spy on each other? Probably for the same reason that the government does it: because we can. The equipment is cheap and quick to install. Perhaps it is simply an extension of the natural curiosity which has us twitching curtains and snooping over the neighbor's fence, but updated for the electronic age.

But at least curtain-twitchers go to bed sometimes, unlike surveillance equipment. That so many of us are willing to become members of "the extended police family" doesn't exactly boost confidence in the strength of modern communities. And of course, it gives the state all the legitimacy it needs to carry on with its own surveillance.

CHAPTER NINETEEN

ME AND MY CONCLUSIONS

"If you've got nothing to hide, you've got nothing to fear."

— Frequent response to those who express concern about the growth of the surveillance society.

Maybe so, but is there really anyone out there with nothing to hide? At the risk of sounding like some 1960s psychotherapist, is there anyone who can honestly say that if every moment of their life had been recorded on camera and was analyzed by a team of CCTV operators they would not be deeply embarrassed, almost certainly liable for a few fines—and quite possibly looking at a year or two in the slammer?

The desire sometimes to seek privacy, to creep away from public view and even to do the odd thing we know we shouldn't really do, is a basic human need. Indeed it is recognized in the European Convention on Human Rights, even if that charter, incorporated into British law in 2000, is often overruled. It is that little freedom—to say, clear off, we just want to be on our own—that the surveillance society attacks. Even ignoring some of the concerns which this book has raised—the waste, the possibility of miscarriages of justice, the risk that information might be misused—this would be reason enough to object to the scale of surveillance in modern life.

Thankfully, the ultimate surveillance society, where everyone and everything is watched and listened to all the time, and can be reviewed if anyone wants to, is likely to remain pie in the sky. As has become clear during my researches, authorities are already struggling sensibly to use the CCTV cameras and other surveillance equipment that they have already installed. Much of it doesn't work very well. That which does work often doesn't tell authorities anything particularly useful. In fact, the excessive collection of data tends to act as a fog through which authorities struggle to find what they are looking more. The more Big Brother watches us, the less he seems to see.

For this reason, it is sometimes hard to take the surveillance society seriously. Quite often it seems more like a bad joke. We see the CCTV cameras and sense an atmosphere of control, but the more familiar we become with them the more we realize they are being watched by a bored operative who has probably fallen asleep or gone for a pee. And anyway, what are they supposed to do when a hooded lout breaks a window, then flicks an up-yours sign at the cameras? I wouldn't be at all surprised if in a few years' time many towns in Britain, the CCTV capital of the world, come to same conclusion as the authorities in Melbourne, Australia: take the damn things down and spend the money on real police officers.

On other occasions, the sinister side of the surveillance society is only too evident. From the retention of Google search records to Britain's national DNA database, the amount of information now gathered on us, and the speed with which it can be retrieved by law enforcement agencies, or by criminals, is extraordinary. Its potential for misuse is horrible. For most of us this will seem a vague threat—until the day we are turned down for a job on the basis of mistaken information gathered on us via the internet, or the day bailiffs arrive at our house demanding payment for goods bought by someone who stole our identity. Then we will be in the thick of it—and find that the way out is tortuous. It is a bitter irony that excessive information-gathering has hugely increased the opportunities for fraud—particularly for users of credit cards—and yet when the defrauded try to report crimes they often find the police don't want to know. What can one do other than to tear up one's credit cards and advertise the fact, as I am doing here, that I do not have a credit card, I do not want a credit card, I never will have a credit card—and that anyone who produces one in my name is attempting to defraud me.

It is all too easy to make a mental link between the electronic surveillance of modern Western democracies, Britain especially, and the autocracies of the old Soviet bloc. Yet for all our attachment to Big Brother and his mysterious electronic presence, the autocracies of Communist Europe were not based on electronic surveillance. Far from it. It wasn't smart cameras and talking lamp-posts which kept an eye on citizens of the Soviet bloc, but a vast army of human agents. The Stasi, the East German secret police force, for example, had 90,000 agents, who infiltrated every neighborhood, every organization. It is a world away from the remote surveillance society of modern Britain, where the "spies" have been banished to remote CCTV control rooms. The Stasi was malign and ultimately unable to prevent East German citizens from fleeing—the trigger for the collapse of the nation—but no one can deny that as a surveillance society it worked. It genuinely kept an eye on individuals. If Western democracies wanted to create effective surveillance societies, they would do well to learn a lesson from the Soviet bloc, and recruit humans, rather than machines, to do the spying. But of course, Western democracies do not really want to do this. In the battle between freedom and surveillance, freedom often does eventually win. It is remarkable how often, from bright yellow speed cameras to the rules concerning the use of telephone taps in court, surveillance is undermined by laws passed to protect the privacy of the public, sometimes absurdly so.

Of one thing I am sure: the surveillance society is to some extent a product of laziness and penny-pinching on the part of law enforcement agencies. How much cheaper, how much more comfortable and safe for those expected to do the work, that a boisterous town center be monitored from a centrally-heated control room full of screens than by sending police officers out on the street. In Britain, at least, the growth of CCTV and traffic enforcement cameras has coincided with a fall in the number of patrols by real, living police officers. Electronic surveillance is not always augmenting traditional policing; it is more often than not replacing it, with poor results. As the reformed shoplifter invited back to test the effectiveness of CCTV cameras in shops said: "I've never known one leap off the wall and nick anyone."

The escalation in the use of CCTV and other forms of electronic surveillance is also about buck-passing. It is a means for public authorities to make some kind of response to complaints over rising crime. You want to know what we are doing about the drunken violence outside your front door every Friday and Saturday night? We're installing CCTV, that's what. You don't understand exactly how it works or what it does, and we're not going to show you if you ask. But we're counting on the fact that it all sounds jolly technological and gives the impression that everything is under control, when in fact we know deep down that all this gadgetry, like Southend Pier itself, is a dead end.

The surveillance society often struggles to catch criminals, but what it does magnificently well is to create offences. The government comes up with a compulsory ID card scheme? It struggles to explain how it will prevent crime, but at a stroke it has made criminals out of the many people who will refuse to take out a card or who will forget to update theirs. It is truly depressing how government so often fails to anticipate the effects of surveillance. For example, British householders have begun to be issued with trashcans (for domestic waste) fitted with microchips. The aim of this exercise is one day to establish a system that charges householders per unit of weight of rubbish they discard. It is so obvious what will happen as a result that one wants to scream: in nice, middle class neighborhoods people will dutifully pay their bills, while public-housing projects and the countryside will quickly become submerged beneath mountains of litter as residents seek to evade the charges, and fail to be caught (just try reporting a case of illegal dumping to your local council and I guarantee nothing will happen because of a "shortage of resources"). Of course, it costs money to collect waste and it is only fair that those who dispose of it should pay for it. But why can't we do the obvious: charge a deposit on food packaging, and all other goods, based on the environmental cost of disposing of it—then effectively refund the deposit in the form of a free waste collection service?

Big Brother is only going to get more nosey...

In its report on the surveillance society published in 2006, the Information Commissioner's office painted a grim portrait of life in 2016, by which time much of the surveillance technology that at present is science fiction or in the early stages of development will have become a reality. It imagines, for example, the Jones family who "have chips implanted in their arms to enable cashless shopping." No more credit card misery—when the Joneses want to buy something they merely run their wrists over a scanner and the money is deducted straight from their account.

Then there is the family's 74-year-old granny, Greta, who lives alone in a spartan room at the Sunnyview Retirement Home, so mollycoddled by technology that none of her family feel the need to go and see her any more. If Greta fails to move around her apartment for an hour or two, motion-detectors alert medical staff to the possibility that she has keeled over. Her heartbeat is monitored constantly and every time she visits the lavatory her blood sugar is monitored so that her doctor knows if she is developing diabetes. All the food in her fridge, meanwhile, is fitted with radio frequency identity tags, so that when she runs low on milk or butter an order will be dispatched to the local supermarket, which will deliver the item without her needing to go shopping. Or at least it will if the order is not intercepted by the government's health police who, studying all the medical and dietary data collected from Greta and her peers, will be able to bombard her with healthy eating advice.

And so it goes on.

Yuck, yuck, yuck. Of course, all these things would be dreadful. But I am not sure I can take this picture of life in 2016 seriously. Having studied how the surveillance society works in practice I have a suspicion that life might end up just a little more like this:

For the Jones family the final straw comes when Mrs. Jones tries to pay for little Toby's sneakers—and has her left arm rejected at the till. "I'm sorry, Mrs. Jones," comes the robotic voice from the automated shop assistant, "but your arm expired two months ago." Alarmed, Mrs. Jones pathetically offers her right arm instead. Beep.... beep! "I'm sorry, but your right arm is overdrawn."

Oh yes, of course, how silly of Mrs. Jones to forget: she has run up a large overdraft paying Greta's rent after she begged to be removed from the Sunnyview Retirement Home. She had been left exhausted by the paramedics rushing in every half an hour during her customary afternoon nap. She had been getting pretty damned tired, too, of being inundated with blueberry yogurt. In fact, the blueberry yogurts made her so angry that several members of staff had had to go on sick leave, worn down by Greta's heart monitor screaming in their office all the time. She hated blueberry yogurt, but what could she do? She had bought one once, thinking the picture looked nice on the top, had taken one mouthful, thrown it away—only for the supermarket to deliver another. She had thrown that one away, too, but it had been replaced almost immediately. She could never seem to get through on the customer care number, and so those yogurts just kept on coming—at such a frequency that the supermarket had picked her out for a special Christmas deal: a hamper full of them.

And don't let us even get started on what happens when Greta is bashed over the head bang in front of a CCTV camera outside the Sunnyview Retirement Home—and police regretfully inform her that her attackers cannot be traced because the footage is blurred, and no they can't put an advert in the local paper asking whether anyone recognizes her attackers from the picture because it could potentially infringe their privacy...

I have examined the surveillance society as best I can, without hacking into the government's computers. I know that I can tolerate many things. I can suffer the CCTV cameras, I can stomach credit agencies snooping on my shopping habits. I dare say that when I am forced to take out an ID card I will grudgingly submit to that too. When the police are granted powers to take DNA samples from absolutely anyone they like, I will do my best to pervert the system by rubbing my hands on the family cat first, but I suspect I will eventually fall into line.

But on one thing I draw the line. When the government calls me in to have a microchip implanted under my skin, I'm not going. If the time comes when we are treated like groceries in a supermarket distribution center, that's it. I will be going underground, or rather taking to the hills and forests where I will hunt, scavenge—and officially cease to exist. I may even see you there.

Appendix

I am indebted to the British Library for allowing me to view the typescript of *2007*, George Orwell's unfinished sequel to *1984*, written after he had had second thoughts as to how a surveillance society would really function. Here is published an extract for the very first time.

It was a bright cold day in April, and Winston Smith, now 62, hobbled up the steps of Victory Mansions. He had been waiting for 23 years for an operation on his varicose veins, and the post had brought bad news. "Due to information we have received," read the letter from the local NHS Trust, "we have concluded that your eating habits would not be conducive to your recovery from this operation, and therefore it must be postponed until you can prove that you have increased your intake of fruit and vegetables."

Winston swore beneath his breath. It had been a dreadful mistake, he realized, to have taken out his loyalty card at Asbos supermarket. His shopping habits must have been fed through to the giant NHS computer housed in the shiny building of the Ministry of Five-a-Day, which he could see half a mile away over the rooftops. From there, the information must have been matched up with his medical records, and an automatic letter had been generated to cancel his operation. A shudder of fear went through him. But what if the information was then matched up against his "five-a-day" card, the cards which all citizens had to carry in the pockets to prove that they were consuming five portions of fruit and vegetables every day? He knew full well that he had faked some of the entries, like claiming he had eaten a pomegranate two days earlier. And that could only mean one thing: when the computer discovered the discrepancy between his shopping habits and the information on his "five-a-day card," his name would automatically be added to the Unhealthy Eaters' Database. Every mealtime for the next five years he would now be obliged to report to the Party canteen, where a fruit and vegetable officer would select his meal for him.

But when Winston read further, he realized that something far worse lay in store. "We have also reason to believe that you have been smoking," the letter went on to say. "You will be contacted over the next few days by an anti-smoking officer." He froze with fear. That could only mean one thing: he must attend one of the compulsory smoking-cessation courses in the Welsh mountains. But there must have been a dreadful mistake: he had last smoked over 20 years ago, after suffering a coughing fit during the Physical Jerks. How come the computer had mistaken him for an active smoker? There was only conclusion: that somebody had faked his "five-a-day" card and, when caught with a cigarette, had shown it to the anti-smoking police. But now the wrong-doing was registered in his name.

He ran fast from his flat, down the dingy corridor to the single public telephone installed in Victory Mansions. He must try at once to try to reach the Smoking Cessation Hotline and plead with them that there had been an error. But he knew that his chances were slim. As he reached the ground floor he ran into a long line of people. It was the queue which always formed in the mornings as residents attempted to get through to various government hotlines, to correct the information that Big Brother had held on them. At the head of the queue was a prole mindlessly humming Vivaldi to herself as she waited to reach the right department of the Ministry of Transportation. A few minutes later her singing had given way to sobbing. It was no use: however much she pleaded that she had never been to Nottingham, where two days earlier a street camera had apparently caught her jaywalking in front of a Party officer's car, the automated call center refused to believe her. Citizens were always falling foul of the facial-recognition cameras that had been installed all over the cities of Airstrip One. But there was nothing anyone could do about them.

Winston could wait no longer. In three minutes' time, he realized, he would have to be upstairs in his flat, in front of the Telescreen for the Five Minutes' Humiliation. He couldn't stand the program himself, but many people enjoyed watching it. It revolved around a house-full of proles who humiliated themselves by performing menial tasks for Big Brother. Then, citizens were forced to vote on who should be purged from Big Brother's house. Why was there never any shortage of volunteers for this filthy spectacle, wondered Winston? Bizarrely, perhaps the proles actually enjoyed appearing on it.

Just at that moment his attention was grabbed by a voice coming from the telescreen. "Pay attention," said a child's voice. "It's voting time." Winston sat bolt upright and pretended to concentrate. Then the voice continued: "Come on, pay attention number 4657385 Wilbert Smith." Wilbert Smith? Winston sighed with relief: it wasn't him whom was being reprimanded after all: the telescreen must be malfunctioning again, and broadcasting messages to entirely the wrong people. Was it safe to turn the machine down, and get on with something else? Just then, the telescreen blinked and went dead. Once more Winston Smith felt a warm surge of relief. The telescreen almost certainly wouldn't be mended that evening, which meant he could safely go for a walk.

He had walked no more than 10 yards from the front door of Victory Mansions when he suffered a bang to the head, and fell to the ground. As he fell, his attacker reached inside his pocket for his wallet, and then ran off. This was always happening, cursed Winston. In fact it was the second time in a week. Dazed, he picked himself up. He knew there was no point in reporting the incident. Somehow, the telescreens never seemed to be watching when there were Muggers about. Or if they were, the photographs they took were too fuzzy for the criminals to be recognized. Were the Muggers a sinister force employed by Big Brother to raise money in order to pay for the five year plan? Winston didn't know. All he did know was that he had a very sore head, he was in so much pain that he couldn't move—and that the bleeper in his pocket was going off: reminding him that it was time to return to Victory Mansions for the citizens daily toenail inspection...

INDEX